TNT
The Power Within You

Also by

Claude Bristol

The Magic of Believing

TNT
The Power Within You

How to Release the Forces Inside You
—and Get What You Want!

by

Claude M. Bristol

and

Harold Sherman

A FIRESIDE BOOK
Published by Simon & Schuster
New York London Toronto Sydney

FIRESIDE
Simon & Schuster Building
Rockefeller Center
1230 Avenue of the Americas
New York, New York 10020

First Fireside Edition 1992

Published in 1987 by Prentice Hall Press
Originally published by Prentice-Hall, Inc.

FIRESIDE and colophon are registered
trademarks of Simon & Schuster Inc.

Manufactured in the United States of America

41 43 45 47 49 50 48 46 44 42

Library of Congress Catalog Card Number: 54-5668
ISBN-13: 978-0-671-76546-0
ISBN-10:   0-671-76546-9

CONTENTS

moping! Prepare yourself to face anything! Abandon all limited thinking! Stop kidding yourself!

CONTENTS

moping! Prepare yourself to face anything! Abandon all limited thinking! Stop kidding yourself!

CONTENTS

TNT
The Power Within You

1

"THAT SOMETHING"
WITHIN CALLED T N T

For those of you who seek to learn and make progress, I gently lay this message in your laps. I do so without the slightest fear but that it will turn your world entirely upside down—bringing you health, wealth, success and happiness, provided you understand and accept it.

Remember, T N T is a dangerously high explosive; so when you gather it closely, handle it carefully. Down through the centuries its power has destroyed those who sought to misuse it. Therefore exercise great caution that it is used only for good.

This power can be proved by the teachings of the Bible, certain well-established laws of physics, and, last but not least, just plain common sense. Read and determine for yourself whether or not the proofs I offer stand by themselves.

Some of you may see only the spiritual side, others recognize the scientific truths, and still others may accept it as just a practical operating device to put you on the road to success. No matter: many know the truth, and for you who will open your minds the light will pour in with dazzling white brilliancy.

I'm indebted to an old friend of mine, an expert on X-ray and electrical high frequency apparatus, who, when I was a boy experimenting with electricity, called to my attention the first bit of powerful TNT in my pocket. Then I didn't know what it was and didn't understand, but fortunately it has remained there all through the years.

As I look back, I realize why he didn't force me to understand what it was. He believed in me, and knew that when I was ready to accept it, I would. It's taken nearly thirty years, during which time I sought up and down the highways, looking, seeking and searching for "that something"—the *secret*—TNT.

All the time there was some in my pocket, mine for the mere reaching. However, I've got a firm grip on it now, and I will divide it graciously, knowing that if used wisely it will blow away all obstacles and straighten out the road on which you've been wanting to travel all your life.

Why are you blocked?

For many years I was a newspaper man, frequently behind the scenes. I met great men and women, interviewed famous people. Naturally, I studied them and tried to understand what peculiar qualities they possessed that placed them above the others. But their secret evaded me.

Then came the First World War and I wondered

why others made progress while I seemed to be blocked in my own ambitions. The war did teach me, however, that I could sleep in the mud, eat moldy bread and live to laugh about it. This is part of my T N T, so remember what I learned. It helped me to give Old Man Fear a solar-plexus blow, and I believe it will help you.

Hoping to find a royal road to fortune, I read hundreds of the so-called "success" books, but they took me nowhere. I did the same with books on philosophy, psychology, and still the great secret kept just a jump ahead of me. I joined secret fraternal organizations, hoping that I might find that which I sought. However, just like the bit of T N T in my pocket, the secret was in every book, in the great orders, everywhere, in fact, right under my very nose, but something kept me from it.

You will have to determine for yourself what keeps *you* from it if you don't get it from T N T. It's there. If you don't find it in the printed word, look between the lines—as I've done my best to present it to you.

Are you afraid?

Following the war, I became a member of a coast-wide investment banking organization, and during the years I cherished quite a dream—as did thousands of others in all lines of business—only to discover that the air castles which I built were on an unstable foundation.

That cataclysmic happening which turned the world upside down financially obliterated my air castles entirely, and I became afraid. I got lost in the fog. Everywhere I turned, something fell in on me.

As an executive of the organization, my responsibilities multiplied. Our business, owing to the economic changes which were taking place in the world, faced a crisis. Many people, failing to understand the catastrophe which had overtaken business everywhere, were critical. All of this brought worry and many sleepless nights. I found myself dreading to go to work, fearing that each day would bring added misery.

The weeks went on and conditions got worse and worse. I was baffled. Several times I talked about getting out of the business; and one day, in the latter part of June, 1931, I made up my mind to leave. I mentioned this to one of the women with whom I had been associated in business for several years and saw nothing but reproach in her eyes

That night I tried to sleep. Again, I found it impossible. I paced the floor for hours—when at about 3:30 in the morning I suddenly stopped and sat down. I was face to face with myself. I could follow the inclination to run and leave the others to carry on by themselves, or I could stay and do my share; a duty which I knew was mine.

I caught myself saying, almost aloud:

"*Right is right. It's always been right. It can't be otherwise.*" This was something I had been taught since infancy.

Suddenly there appeared to be an unfoldment!

Out of the air!

Out of the air came a voice saying:

"*What have you been looking for all these years? What were you taught? What did you learn? Where have you been? Where are you going?*"

14

I jumped to my feet, crying: "I know it. I've got it now. It's the secret. That's what they tried to teach me. It is the Royal Secret, too!"

Something told me that I would find those identical words in a book which had been given me many years before and which I had tried to read, failed to understand and had put aside. It was written by a great man, Albert Pike, a mystic, a poet and a scholar. Pulling it from the shelf, feverishly I ran through the pages. The words were there and I understood immediately.

Open your mind

I now had the key. I could see a broad smooth highway and at the end of that highway, a perfect flood of gorgeously beautiful radiance:

"That's the road you are on now. What a simpleton you have been! They tried to teach you, they tried to help you and you kept your mind closed—thinking that you alone could find the road and stay on it."

I was nearly overcome with the sheer joy of it all. My fears, my worries had disappeared. I smiled. I knew that I was right and that everything would be right for me from then on. I slept like a baby.

There was a different atmosphere in the office that day. The oppressive black clouds which hung over us began to fade away. I told the woman—she with the reproachful eyes—what had happened, and she smiled a knowing smile. She helped me get back on the track, and I can never repay her.

As one learned man said: "All of us are born with the ability to differentiate between right and wrong, and with the ability to achieve, but some of us must run head-on into a stone wall, smash ourselves to bits before we really know what it's all about."

I hit the wall with a terrific crash and it was the greatest thing, the finest thing, that ever happened to me.

Many, noting the transformation, asked for an explanation. I told some of my closest friends. Knowing it will help, I give it to all of you.

Tap–Tap–Tap!

Take a little at a time. Like a little drop of water, tap—tap—tap, TNT will wear away your old fears and doubts and prejudices, making room for new ideas, new concepts, new truths.

Tap–tap–tap: it is opportunity knocking at the door of your mind. Open up your mind and let this knowledge in.

From the day I decided to pass on this charge of TNT to others, it has been put to use by thousands of individuals, firms and organizations. In addition, I have talked and lectured, in person and over the radio, to many additional thousands; and I am very happy to say that, without exception, phenomenal results have been obtained by those who have understood and applied the principles and mechanics outlined herein.

Tap–Tap–Tap!

You may get it all at once, or it may take you a little time to prepare your mind so that the power you've always had can work through you. But don't work at it too hard, don't try to force it. Be assured, the power is there and you can learn to use it.

At the time my awakening came, the morale of our whole organization was at its lowest ebb. Everyone was discouraged. Afraid. By the very necessity of things, we *had* to do an about-face.

Right is right

My job was doing everything I could to help the other fellow because I knew it was right. At first I was perplexed as to the methods I should employ to help others, but I used my own system in calling upon the subconscious, and the inner voice said that I should talk to them.

Some were skeptical, but I said to myself: *"I can prove that I am right!"* And during the week that followed I spent every waking hour reviewing the books that I had studied through the years. Naturally, the Bible came first; then followed studies in Yogism, the philosophies of the old Greek and Roman masters and of the later-day teachers and students. Again I deliberated over the *Meditations* of Marcus Aurelius, reread Thomas Jay Hudson's *Law of Psychic Phenomena* and another book, *The Gist of It,* written by a brilliant physician, Haydon Rochester. Once more, I studied my books on physics, electricity, and those on the vibrations of light, and discovered that not only was I right, as I knew I would be, but that peculiarly the same general basic principles ran through them all. I reread numerous books on psychology and found the same story everywhere. Subsequently,

I quoted excerpts, and lo and behold, things began to move!

Where is your niche?

As I looked about me I made the significant observation that men and women who use this power are showmen, or to use the words of my newspaper days, *headliners,* those who hit the front page. Something causes them to toss away the bushel basket under which they hide their heads, and they rise above the commonplace.

Not that you may ever want to become a headliner in this sense, but you will surely agree that such people who have developed the power within to the *nth* degree have become headliners, or they would never have gotten their niche in the hall of fame. It doesn't follow that they are newspaper publicity-seekers, because some of them are very reticent—and possibly by their very reticence are showmen. (Page Greta Garbo!) Others adopt certain peculiarities or use certain devices to make them stand out from their fellow men. Some wear an efficacious smile (Dwight D. Eisenhower, for one!), others scowl (John L. Lewis!), some command attention by critical barbs at peoples and customs (George Bernard Shaw!), and still others have a certain charm of manner (Eleanor Roosevelt). Long hair (many musicians and conductors such as Leopold Stokowski), whiskers and sideburns (the Smith Brothers!), monocles (Charles Coburn) play their part. Flowing robes and distinctive dress are worn by others (Mark Twain and his famous white suits!). The showmanship of some is evidenced by red neckties, others by spats, affected manners, and some even by their number of marriages and divorces (such as Tommy Manville!)

The world takes note of the unorthodox, the unconventional, the uninhibited individuals, and most headliners come under these classifications. They are different in some one or more particulars. Some deliberately flaunt and dramatize their differences. Others are not concerned with what people think about them. They are too busy being themselves and doing what they want in life, whether or not it is making right use of their power of T N T.

Many master the art of oratory, the science of warfare, banking, statesmanship, politics, the arts; but all of them stand out in the full glare of the spotlight—as headliners.

The number is legion. I mention a few of those of history and today: Demosthenes, Nero, Julius Caesar, Christopher Columbus, Galileo, Cleopatra, Balzac, de Maupassant, Sir Isaac Newton, Joan of Arc, Cromwell, Edgar Allan Poe, Benjamin Franklin, Alexander Hamilton, Bismarck, Alexander Graham Bell, General Grant, Abraham Lincoln, Cecil Rhodes, P. T. Barnum, Clemenceau, Lord Kitchener, Woodrow Wilson, Sir Thomas Lipton, Mussolini, Hitler, Winston Churchill, Joseph Stalin, Lenin, Franklin D. Roosevelt, Charles E. Hughes, Lloyd George, Mahatma Gandhi, Will Rogers, Douglas Fairbanks, Henry Ford, Thomas Edison, John Burroughs, Charles Lindbergh, Alfred E. Smith, Jane Addams, George Washington Carver, Al Jolson, Eleanor Roosevelt, Marion Anderson, Ralph Bunche, Harry Truman, Jawaharlal Nehru, Dwight D. Eisenhower, Ezio

Pinza, Bernard Baruch, Jimmy Stewart, Jane Froman, Cecil B. DeMille, Albert Einstein and Dr. Albert Schweitzer.

You could go on and on, each name calling to mind a personality, living or dead, who has been unique in expression and achievement. Such individuals have been and are found in every walk of life. It will always be so, as their use of the power within elevates them to the top in their profession or endeavor.

You will note the inclusion of such names as Nero, Julius Caesar, Mussolini, Hitler, Stalin and Lenin in this list. They were all brilliant in their way, and attained their positions of great power through use of "that some-, thing" within—but they trampled humanity in the dust doing it. As history evaluates them, it must weigh the evil they have done against the good. You can become a headliner by using this inner power wrongly as well as rightly. That's why it's so wonderful and so dangerous at the same time! That's why you must learn how to control it, in a way helpful to you and to others—and (if you become a headliner), to the world!

Gandhi used this power, I am sure, and I think he was perhaps the greatest headliner of modern times. You can find many pictures showing him in the civilized garb of present-day man, but in his later years he kept his hair cropped short, wore only a loincloth and a pair of huge spectacles. I have no right to say that Gandhi affected this attire for any specific purpose, but I believe he did it with the realization that this appearance helped focus the world's attention upon himself for India's cause.

I make no attempt to explain why those who use this power are showmen. But you'll notice, as you begin to exercise this power in your own life, that it will make you stand out among your friends and loved ones. They will immediately detect a difference in you, the way you express yourself, the way you act. This doesn't mean that you will be showing off or trying to attract attention. It just means that you are starting, for the first time, perhaps, to be really yourself, to take advantage of the opportunities that are all about you, to cut loose from your old hidebound ideas and limitations, and to claim that which is rightfully yours—which you might have attained long ago, had you understood how to release the power of T N T in your life.

Remember: you can't be a shrinking violet and win any recognition or respect for yourself in this world.

"A city that is set upon a hill cannot be hid. Neither do men light a candle and place it under a bushel. . . ."

Again:

"The great truths of life become known only to those who are prepared to accept them. . . ."

Thousands who used the power within for evil brought on their own destruction. Look back through history and you can pick these men and women out for yourself.

We get out of life exactly what we put into it—no more, no less. This is an old truism, but it cannot be emphasized enough. When we put in good thoughts, constructive efforts, and do good, then we receive like in return, for

"Whatsoever a man soweth, that shall he also reap."

What *is* "that something"—the T N T that rocks the earth? The power within every and any individual which he *has* to use, if he is to amount to anything in life!

21

Have you figured it out yet? It's you, your real self, the hidden power of your own *inner mind*, released under purposeful control, and directed to serve you in the meeting of any experience, the removal of any obstacle and the overcoming of any condition, economic, physical, mental or spiritual.

Picture the force!

It is the explosive force of a mental picture of what you want in life, given by you to your subconscious, touched off by faith in yourself and faith in God.

Whatever you picture, within reason, can come true in your life *if* you have sufficient faith in the power within!

That's your TNT—a mental image of what you want and the faith that you can and will get it!

It's as simple as that: so simple that millions of men and women won't *believe* it, won't take the time to learn about this power, would rather go on beating their heads against stone walls of willful blindness, ignorance and stubbornness, and keep on creating all manner of misery, economic loss and ill health for themselves through wrong thinking.

Remember, I stumbled along for thirty years with a bit of TNT in my pocket. All I had to do was reach for it, and I had hold of a power which could have saved me worlds of grief. But I knew more than the happy, successful men and women around me who were using this power and who were inviting me to share it. I thought I could do it all myself, that this success business was largely luck, that you couldn't depend on faith or any

God Power. I was exposed to this truth, time and time again, but it didn't take. I had vaccinated myself against it by my skeptical, scoffing attitude.

Let's hope you don't get as sick of life and as despondent and despairing as I was before you clean out the pockets of your mind and find the T N T that's waiting for you there.

What's that? You say you've come across a *detonating cap* already? Good! Get it set. Put out the caution signals. Proceed carefully and prepare yourself for the first *explosion* in your consciousness which is going to blast away your wrong thinking and open up a new pathway that will change the course of your entire life—for the better!

2

WHAT "THAT SOMETHING" HAS DONE FOR OTHERS

*Nothing in this world is
so powerful as an idea
whose time has come.*
VICTOR HUGO

The time has come for the greatest idea in the world to take possession of your consciousness. It is a simple idea, but when you open up your mind and let it in, you'll never be the same again. Like TNT it will rock the earth around you and beneath you. It will shake you to the foundations of your being. It will destroy old false concepts and replace them with new ones. It will eventually remove fear and worry from your life. It will release you from chronic nervous tensions, chase the butterflies out of your stomach, restore your self-confidence, give you a more positive attitude, and enable you to face things you've been running away from, for years!

All the great, successful men and women in this world have made use of this idea. It has been the dominant idea in their lives. Without it they could never have been great, in their way, or successful.

What *is* this idea?

It is the realization that *what you picture in your mind, if you picture it clearly and confidently and persistently enough, will eventually come to pass in your life!*

That's it! Oh, of course, there's a little more to it than that. But boiled down to the very essence, the wise men said it all when they said: "As a Man thinketh in his mind and in his heart so is he!"

Get it? "As a man pictures in his mind and in his heart—so is he!"

When this idea first hit me it knocked me down for the count. It was a real haymaker, because I had been blaming the other fellow, circumstances beyond my control, for the mess I was in. I just knew I hadn't been responsible for all the unhappy experiences I had undergone. Well, anyway, it helped salve my many hurts to pretend that I hadn't been to blame. But deep down within, I think I had finally begun to realize that the way I thought and felt about things had some connection with what was happening to me.

If I got up in the morning, depressed and convinced it was going to be a bad day, it more often than not turned out a bad day. At first I thought I was "psychic," that I could tell in advance what was going to happen. It took a long time and I took a lot of unnecessary punishment before it dawned on me that there is a universal law in the mental realm, "like always attracts like," and that

I had been creating what happened to me by wrong thinking.

Looking around me, I saw happy men and women to whom happy things were happening. They got up in the morning expecting good things to come to them—and good things did!

Sometimes these happy people had unhappy experiences, but I noticed that they didn't let these experiences get them down. They got up the next day expecting *more* good things to happen, and sure enough *more* good things did!

Before my awakening came, this always amazed me. I even resented it. Why should just a different mental attitude make so much difference?

I didn't know then that there is a mighty force in the world which scientists call electro-magnetism. I didn't know that everything in the universe is electro-magnetic in nature, that the laws of attraction and repulsion operate electro-magnetically; that when you assume a positive or negative attitude of mind, you get a positive or negative result; that there is no such thing as an accident in life—that everything happens in direct accordance with the laws of cause and effect!

Read and reread the above paragraph! Let these facts soak in till you never forget them—because they have the power to change your life!

There is nothing new to what I am telling you, except as it may be new to you. This same message has been written and delivered thousands of times. It runs through the Bible; you find it in the great fraternal orders; it led the Three Wise Men; the Crusaders carried it; every outstanding character of history has used it. Moses, Alexander the Great, Napoleon, Shakespeare, Washington, Lincoln, Benjamin Franklin, Edison, Dr. Steinmetz, Barnum, F. D. Roosevelt and numberless others had a grasp of "that something."

The wisest men of all ages, the "medicine men," religious leaders, great teachers, the Mayan priests, the Yogis, healers and miracle men—all of them knew this secret. Some worked it one way, some another.

They pictured in their minds and hearts what they wanted—and what they pictured eventually came true!

Moses *pictured* leading his people to the Promised Land; Alexander the Great and Napoleon pictured great conquests; Shakespeare pictured the creation of his immortal writings; Washington pictured the winning of independence for the Thirteen Colonies; Lincoln pictured the freeing of the slaves and the preservation of the Union; Benjamin Franklin pictured the capturing of lightning through a kite, as a means of proving that electricity and lightning are the same force; Edison pictured the electric light, moving pictures, the phonograph, the electric train and countless other great inventions; Steinmetz pictured new uses for electric power; Barnum pictured "the greatest show on earth," a circus that would travel around the world by train; Roosevelt pictured leading his country out of its worst depression.

These were great pictures by great and inspired men, and all these pictures, held resolutely in mind and converted into action, were brought to pass by the faith and energy and vision and courage and steadfastness of each individual.

These, and many like them, were just human beings like yourself. If they knew and could achieve, so can you.

Halt! Think! Ponder!

What made these people great? It was that they pictured themselves attaining! They dared to picture great achievement. And the power within, given these pictures to work on, finally brought them into being.

You have to *think* big to *be* big. A small man is made up of small thoughts. He cannot remain small and think big.

Reflect for a moment!

Where did the steamboat, the locomotive, the automobile, the electric light, the sewing machine, the radio, the typewriter and a million other objects and conveniences come from? All were thoughts or mental pictures in the minds of men before they became realities. Everything on this earth, except that which nature creates or has provided, is the result of sustained thought.

Take out of this world everything that has been created by thought alone, and you would have nothing left but the primitive jungle. This is the quickest, most graphic way to give you a comprehension of what the mind of man has done.

When the real history of the evolution of mind is written it will make the greatest, most thrilling story of all time because it will cover all time and every phase of human experience.

This story will tell how man required thousands upon thousands of years to emerge from the depths of ignorance, superstition, fear, prejudice, mythology and wrong concepts.

It will tell of great minds like Galileo, who believed

with Copernicus that the earth moves around the sun, and was compelled by the Inquisition to take back his statements and was forbidden to publish his learned books. With what shame we look back upon such persecutions by the early Church of men who dared pursue the truth despite existing doctrines and decrees.

The history of the human mind will give honor to Charles Darwin, whose profound study of plants and animals led to his famous, world-shaking, *The Origin of Species,* in which he advanced the theory of evolution. To the credit of modern-day theology, God's handiwork in and through evolution is now being recognized by many religious sects.

Time's majestic march through the ages has seen man's mind develop powers he little dreamed of in the early days of his residence on this earth.

Proof that man is more than animal

The fact that the creature man has been able to survive all these centuries in the struggle against all forms of life and in spite of the inhumanities of his fellow man is proof that he possesses superior powers within. Man is a veritable god in the making although he reveals, still too often, devilish tendencies.

It is that inner power which man possesses, beyond and apart from any other living creature on this earth, which has made it possible for him to advance to his present state of development and awareness.

The power within has lifted man above all other animals. While there are probably higher intelligences on other planets and in higher realms of being, it is now evident that man has unlimited potentialities for further development within him. He is just in the kindergarten of his opportunities for unfoldment and achievement, once he learns how to live peacefully and co-operatively with his fellow man. He is in the midst of learning this painful lesson now. But I have faith he is going to learn it. I have faith in this vast inner power, greater than man, of which man is becoming more and more conscious—"that something" which can and will eventually free man from his fears and hates and prejudices—and give him such understanding of his own self that he will, in turn, be able to understand others.

You always know when a man or woman is using the power within his or her life. Such people walk in the consciousness of this power which is in and behind their every thought and act. They are poised, self-assured, courageous, uninhibited and magnetic in expression. They know where they are going and how to get there. They have pictured their future and are moving with resoluteness and conviction into that future. There is a spirit about them which is contagious. They tend to carry you along with them, to spur you on to greater efforts in your own behalf. These people are the *planners* and the *doers* of the world. The great mass of unthinking human beings follow in their wake.

Do you lead the pack, or are you one of the pack? If you are a follower of others, you have not yet discovered "that something" within you. To be a leader, to be able to step out ahead of the pack in your line of work or human interest or expression, you must know how to draw upon the power within. It is absolutely essential. You cannot be anything without it.

The law of attraction will only bring to you what you *picture*. The creative power within must be magnetized by what you visualize for it to do.

Picture! Picture! Picture!

This is the simple command which leads to attainment. Picture! Picture! Picture! But be sure you are picturing what you really want and not developing pictures of fear and worry which will cause that inner power to create for you what you don't want!

If Edison, when he was trying to invent the electric light, had pictured failure instead of success, he would never have made ten thousand experiments before he developed the filament which would carry the electric current and produce light. Think of it! Edison failed 9,999 times before he succeeded once! But each failure taught him what would *not* work, and through the laborious process of elimination finally led him to the discovery of something that *would* work!

How long could you persist in the face of such colossal failure? Edison is credited with saying, "Success is ninety-nine per cent perspiration and one per cent inspiration."

When you know you are working with the power within, as Edison did, your faith will never falter. You will continue the struggle against all obstacles and seeming setbacks, in the unshakeable conviction that you will eventually succeed.

Sometimes, failure to attain a certain goal has led unexpectedly and even more rewardingly to another Consider the famous case of Columbus. His studies convinced him that the world is round, and he believed that by sailing westward he could reach Cathay and the Indies. It took him five years before he was able to get the ships necessary for such a journey. Even then, his crew was so doubtful of his ideas that they mutinied and almost turned back. Still Columbus never lost faith. The power within him kept him going, and when he finally sighted some islands he called them the "West Indies." Even after making three more trips to America, Columbus died without realizing he had discovered a new world! History, however, does not record Columbus as a failure. No good effort is ever lost!

What you picture must come to pass if you picture it long enough, clearly enough and confidently enough. I am going to repeat many of these statements again and again, in different ways, because I want them to be indelibly impressed upon your consciousness.

The successful men and women of the world never lose sight of their *pictures*. They keep on reminding their creative power of what they desire in life so that it will keep on attracting everything they need to materialize what they have pictured.

Example of picture power

Irma and Farley O'Brien are a young couple now living in North Hollywood, California, in "the home of their dreams." It is just the home that they pictured, which they testify came to them as a direct result of visualization.

For months they had tried to find the right home,

had looked in many sections and had enlisted the aid of many real-estate agents. They had seen a number of attractive houses and yards but none possessed that indescribable appeal, that heart-warming something they were seeking in a place they would wish to buy.

Finally, despairing of finding what they wanted by the routine methods, Irma and Farley decided to stop searching. They had learned of a new way to attract to them what they desired—a magical way.

All they had to do was to sit quietly and picture together the exact house that they wanted, in the faith that this home existed somewhere and already belonged to them.

Irma drew out the floor plans for the house. She visualized the surrounding landscape, the garden, the flowers, the patio—everything. Farley and she discussed these plans, agreed upon them, became enthused over them. They had little money to invest in such a home, but they had faith that the resources would also be made available if they pictured what they desired strongly enough and clearly enough and put forth every effort in the direction of their objective.

Irma said to Farley: "I don't want just a house. I want a home that has been built by a couple who loved it as we will love it, the instant we see it. I want a place that has the atmosphere of love in it and around it. I want to feel this love in every room, in the garden, among the flowers. Do you suppose there is such a place?"

"I'm sure there is," said Farley. "There has to be— or you couldn't feel about it as you do."

And so each night, before retiring, Irma and Farley

pictured themselves being led to such a home, wherever it might be. They dropped off to sleep, dreaming of this home, with the expectation of being led to it when the time and conditions were right. They let go of all previous apprehensions that they would not find what they desired. Somehow, some way, they knew that what they were picturing would materialize for them.

One day, some weeks later, Irma and Farley were at a friend's house and Irma felt impelled to tell this friend of "their dream." The friend listened with interest and then said: "You have just described the home of a friend of mine—a man by the name of Mr. Davies, whose wife died a few months ago, shortly after their 'dream home' was completed. Mr. Davies is still living in the home. He has been offered twice what it cost him but he says that he won't sell until he finds a couple who will love this home as much as his wife and he did."

"Please take us to this man," Irma and Farley requested.

When they arrived outside the home in North Hollywood, they stopped and stared, unbelievingly.

"This is it!" they both cried, even before they had stepped across the threshold . . . the house, the yard, the garden, the flowers, the patio . . . their picture had come to life!

And when they met Mr. Davies at the door, the love of this home was in their eyes, and he saw it, and said to them: "I see that you already like this place. Just make yourselves at home. I won't go with you. Take your time. Go wherever you wish. When you have finished, I'll be waiting."

For an hour Irma and Farley lost themselves in their breathless examination of the beautiful premises. It seemed to them as though they had already moved in . . . as though they had been living in this "home of their dreams," as perhaps they had, in the higher, mental sense.

But now, it was time to face reality. It was obvious that this home would cost far more than they could pay, that any down payment would be in excess of their entire resources.

"What shall we do?" Irma said to Farley. "We've found the home we have pictured—but how can it be ours?"

"Our faith has taken us this far," said Farley. "Let's not doubt that it can take us the rest of the way."

They were out in the backyard and now they turned to enter the house. As they did so, Mr. Davies opened the door. He stood quietly, eyeing them.

"Oh, it's wonderful . . . wonderful!" they exclaimed. "Just what we have been wanting! But it appears to be beyond our means."

"Perhaps it may not be," said Mr. Davies. "I have been requesting a large down payment of people to whom I am not interested in selling. But you love this home as my wife and I did. Somehow, I can feel that she would never forgive me if I sold our beautiful home to a couple who did not share our deep feeling for it. You folks know what you can pay—make your own terms."

A deal was arranged and the O'Briens left with the assurance that the "home of their dreams" would now become their real life home.

Even so, the down payment would take all their

available finances, with no resources in sight to complete the purchase.

"Have we let our feelings run away with us?" Irma questioned. "Should we have assumed this big obligation?"

"Everything has worked out so perfectly," said Farley, "I have faith it will keep on working out this way."

And it did! Today their lovely home is bought and paid for.

Yes, that power within always works when you have learned how to utilize it. It works in ways you cannot possibly imagine, when you place your faith in it and do what you feel is right to do in any situation.

In the case of Irma and Farley, like had attracted like. They had been picturing the kind of a home Mr. Davies owned and he had been picturing selling this home to the kind of a couple they were. Such visualizing had drawn them magnetically together through the medium of the friend to whom Irma felt impelled to confess her desire for "the home of her dreams."

The channels through which you may reach your goal are always provided in much the same manner by the power within, when you have pictured what you want, clearly and confidently and persistently, with faith that what you picture can and will be attained.

All that is good and right for you in life can be drawn to you by right thinking. What "that something" has done for others, it can just as easily do for you.

Positive thoughts attract—negative thoughts repel

Check your thinking! Do you believe what has been told you thus far? Does it begin to ring a bell? Can you look back on your life and see how you have attracted good things to you by positive thinking and bad things by negative thinking? If you can, then you are ready to learn what this creative power can do for you!

3

WHAT "THAT SOMETHING" CAN DO FOR YOU

There are thousands, yes, millions of people seeking the secret—the key to health, riches, happiness, contentment and a solution of their problems.

Through the ages many men and women had the secret, used the power; and I am positive you can acquire it too if you'll think as you read, accept and apply the ideas contained herein.

What do you want?

Where are you going?

Answer these two questions and you will give your life purpose and direction. If you don't know what you want or where you are going, you will get next to nothing and end up nowhere. The person who is unsettled in mind is surrounded with unsettled conditions.

Never forget: like always attracts like!

How you are thinking today determines *what* you will be and *where* you will be tomorrow!

Have you ever noticed the indecisive individual? If he is behind the wheel of a car, he is first in one lane and then in another; he slows down to make a turn, then changes his mind and speeds up; he is over-cautious one minute and reckless the next; he doesn't know where he's at or why—and no one else does, either.

That is no way to get any place or do anything worthwhile. If you are unsettled, uncertain, undecided in your thoughts and actions, it is a sure sign that you are not in complete control of your mind and emotions. It is evidence that you have not yet been introduced to this creative power within which can transform your life.

Today there is a superabundance of talk about atomic power. You may notice they always compare what an atom bomb or a hydrogen bomb or a cobalt bomb can do in terms of so many thousand tons of T N T.

When I first discovered this power in me, the power that best described it was T N T. If you have a force in you equal to T N T, you don't need any greater power than that to move the mountains of fear and doubt and worry and tension and inferiority and frustration and hate and greed and prejudice which have been holding you back and weighing you down.

Just light the fuse, by picturing right things happening to you. Then step back and let "that something"— the magnetic creative power within you—take over.

What can it do for you?

You name it—and it can do it! *Name* it, *believe* in it, *picture* it, *work* at it, and this power will attract to you everything you need to accomplish what you desire.

Overcoming handicaps

A friend of mine who stuttered when a boy wanted to be a preacher. He grew up still wanting to be a preacher, but when he confided his desires to friends and loved ones, they either laughed at him or tried to discourage his ambition.

"Better pick up some vocation where you don't have to appear in public," they recommended. "No one will ever listen to you. Why, you can't speak a sentence without difficulty and when you start stammering, it's embarrassing. It takes you half a minute, sometimes, to get a word out."

"But I don't have to be this way all my life," this man insisted. "One of these days I'm going to speak as well as anyone else. I can see myself doing it and I will do it!"

Today this man has a big church on the West coast. He is one of the most convincing and forceful speakers I have ever heard, and you would never know that there was a time when he had such a serious impediment in his speech.

How did he overcome this drawback? By *picturing!* By calling upon that God-given creative power to help him out.

He told me he used to go out into the farmyard and talk for hours to the chickens. He imagined they were people and that he was addressing them. He said, "I seemed to scare them at first, and I guess I did go through a great many contortions, trying to speak without distortion. Sometimes they would eye me curiously, stopping their eating to do it, and I would imagine I was holding their attention by my oratory. Occasionally, they would act as if they were mesmerized, as chickens often do, and I would pretend I was spellbinding them. Gradually, I obtained better and better control of myself, partly through this practice, and partly through gaining an understanding of what had caused me to stutter.

"You see, my father had been a very dominating man. He believed in the old adage, 'a child should be seen but not heard.' He criticized me, as a boy, when I would speak or express my ideas. It made me self-conscious. I became afraid that I would be ridiculed every time I opened my mouth. This caused me to start stuttering. After that, I was reluctant to speak in the presence of anyone, and people didn't want me to try because it distressed them to see me struggle to say what I wanted to say.

"When I found that I could speak, without stammering, in the presence of the chickens and livestock, I developed the confidence that I could speak just as well in the presence of people. This confidence came as the result of a funny idea which occurred to me. I got the idea that all I had to do was to picture people as so many chickens and cows and horses—and, by doing that, I would lose my fear of them.

"It was a boyish concept but it worked. It helped me not to take myself too seriously, to overcome my sense of inferiority and my feeling of self-consciousness. I realized, too, that I had been *picturing* myself unable to talk in the presence of others because I had been afraid of my father's rebukes. As soon as I changed this picture, and asked for the power to express myself without fear, 'that something' took hold of me. I then attracted the experiences and the training which developed me into the preacher I am today—just as I had visualized so many years ago!"

No matter what your seeming handicap, this creative power is ready and waiting to help you overcome it!

Are you preparing your mind for the manifestation of this power in and through you?

How can you believe?

You first have to be convinced that this power isn't freakish, that it is real and dependable, that you'll be able to recognize it when you discover it within you and that you will know how to go about using it.

That's the purpose, of course, of this book—to reveal that creative power to you and to give you the know-how to make it work successfully for you, as it has for thousands of others.

But you who are reading these lines can't sit on the outside looking in and expect to experience the explosive force of this tremendous power in your consciousness. You've got to open up your inner mind and make it receptive, so the TNT you've hidden away there, through wrong thinking and perhaps ignorance of its existence, can come out and start banging away at your self-made obstacles and drawbacks and difficulties and problems.

You lick whatever you're up against in life ... not from without in—but from within out!

Things first happen in the mind before they can happen in the world without!

This is a wallop, the first time you realize it. You

don't make a move, except through your free will choose
so to do. You can't lay this book down unless you make
up your mind to do it first. And you can't enlist the aid
of "that something" within until you remove the restric-
tions you have placed upon it through your wrong thinking.

Don't be discouraged

A good friend of mine, named Jones, had not been
getting anywhere in his chosen field of advertising. He
was just a run-of-the-mill operator. He decided, one day,
that he would have to change all this. He hadn't known
what he really wanted in his line or where he was going,
so he looked around him.

Was there an advertising position that he felt he was
especially qualified to fill? Yes, there was. The advertising
managership of a national publication similar to the
National Geographic—let's call it the *World Travel
Monthly.*

My friend had been a world traveler. He had a "feeling" for this position, he began to "see himself" acting as
advertising manager. He could put real enthusiasm into
such a visualization. As his interest grew in the possible
landing of this job, he made inquiries of the magazine's
owner.

"Sorry. We are well satisfied with our present advertising manager, Mr. Haley. He has been with us many
years and is doing fine work. As far as we are concerned,
he has a life-time position with us."

Such information would have been enough to discourage nine out of ten men—but not Mr. Jones. He felt
himself impelled to say: "That's all right, but I'm so tre-

mendously interested in your publication, and it would give me so much personal satisfaction to be associated with it, even in an unofficial capacity, would you mind if I sat in on your editorial and advertising conferences whenever I can, and made my recommendations from time to time, as though I were a member of your staff, but without pay?"

The proposal was so unusual that it caught the interest of the magazine owner.

"I, personally, would have no objection, if you are that much interested," he told Mr. Jones. "However, you would have to sell this idea to Mr. Haley He might not like to have a man who is interested in his position associating with him in this manner. But if he is willing to have you devote such spare time as you have to our interests, without any obligation on our part, you are welcome to do so."

Mr. Jones called upon Mr. Haley. The two men took an immediate liking to each other. A warm friendship sprang up, which continued through eight years, during which time Mr. Jones made himself of great value to the *World Travel Monthly* and became conversant with every phase of its operation while he occupied himself with other advertising interests which made him a living.

Finally, there came a day when Mr. Haley was offered a position in California and decided for health and personal reasons, having always wished to reside in this state in his later life, that he would resign from the *World Travel Monthly* and go West.

Mr. Jones is today the advertising manager of the *World Travel Monthly*, having stepped into Mr. Haley's position with full knowledge of it—a position he pictured himself occupying for eight years and worked at all that time!

You still think that inner power can't bring you what *you* want?

What inspiration can do

Do you feel despondent, hopeless, like ending it all? That's how H. C. Mattern felt, some years ago. He had come to New York City from his home in Pennsylvania which he had left because of family and economic troubles. He had hoped to get back on his feet in New York but things, as they often do, when you are upset, mentally and emotionally, had gone from bad to worse.

Mattern finally decided, since he owed seven weeks' room rent, was down to his last couple of dollars, and had exhausted prospects and resources, that the only way out was suicide. But there were several little errands he was intent on doing first, and one of them led him through the book department on the ground floor of Macy's department store. As he passed a booktable the title of a book caught his eye and challenged him. The title was *Your Key to Happiness*, by Harold Sherman.

In Mattern's disturbed state of mind, this title acted as a red rag is supposed to react upon a bull. Mattern raged to himself: "There's no such thing as a *key* to happiness!" But the title stayed with him as he reached the sidewalk, like the lance of a bullfighter stuck in his side. On impulse, he wheeled about, retraced his steps, went back to the booktable, took up the book and bought it with his last remaining dollars.

Returning to his room, with the poison he had also

purchased to take his life, Mattern thumbed through the book in a defiant mood. One of the first passages he came across spoke to him in these words:

"Whether you realize it or not, you are directly or indirectly responsible for everything that happens to you!"

Mattern almost threw the book out the window. He had been blaming his unhappy experiences in life upon others, telling himself that circumstances beyond his control had brought these desperate conditions upon him. The last person he wanted to face was himself, least of all to have to admit that he may have been the cause of any of his shortcomings or problems.

To prove that the author of *Your Key to Happiness* didn't know what he was talking about, Mattern read further. But, the further he read, the harder he found himself being hit.

"You may be wondering, at this very moment, whether there is any real way out of the difficulties which surround you. And, if you are, my answer to you is: Don't lose hope! There is a way to solve your problems— to relieve the conditions which may now be pressing in upon you; a way that will enable you to achieve the things in life which mean most to you. . . ."

Mattern picked up interest. His thoughts of suicide began to recede into the background of his mind. What *was* this way? How could he ever pull himself out of the tailspin he was in?

There it was, in plain black and white:

"You must develop the ability to picture clearly in your mind whatever success you desire."

Remember, I've told you that this message isn't new

—that it has been written and delivered thousands of times; but it is always new to the man or woman who receives it for the first time.

Harold Sherman was telling Mattern just what I am telling you about the power within. Sherman had discovered that power in *his* way, as I had discovered it in *my* way—and we both were given the urge to "tell the world about it."

But Mattern had to be shown; he had to reason it out, every step had to appeal to his logic. He wasn't going to be fooled by nice words or promises. He had become too disillusioned, too far gone, to hit any come-back trail unless he could blaze it himself. But as he dug into the contents of this little book, things began to make sense that had never made sense before. He commenced to review his life in the light of the understanding he was now getting about the operation of his own mind and emotions. He could begin to see how many of his wrong thoughts had attracted wrong results to him. And when he came to the passage where Sherman states that an individual can learn to capitalize upon his failures of the past, that he can extract constructive lessons from them, and that every individual possesses some hidden resources and talents which can be crystallized and developed to pull him out of an economic crisis, Mattern asked himself: "What have I ever done which I can turn to now—and realize money on?"

He thought back through his life and reflected, sadly, that he had been a jack-of-all-trades, a master of none. There didn't seem to be any combination of skills and talents he could call upon to aid him in his extremity. But, wait a minute! Some years ago, he had tried to develop a chemical formula for cleaning and preserving leather upholstered furniture. He had mixed different ingredients together and had come close to a satisfactory solution, but had finally given up the project. Perhaps, if he renewed his efforts in this direction . . . !

Then—*wham*—it happened. Out of the blue, straight from his subconscious, as though handed him on a platter, came the formula he had been seeking! The instant he received it, he *knew* it would work! This was it!

At two o'clock in the morning, H. C. Mattern shelved all plans for leaving this world! Instead, he began making plans for getting hold of the necessary chemicals as soon as the stores opened later in the day, for preparing the solution and finding a buyer for his services in cleaning and preserving leather upholstered furniture!

All doubts were gone and new faith in himself and God had been born. There was a key to happiness and he had found it!

Mattern knew in that moment that this formula had been prepared for him by "that something," the creative power within, in answer to his previous desires and efforts. The only mistake he had made was giving up too soon. But this formula, once created, had been held for him, in his subconscious.

Later in the morning, a new and vitalized Mattern visited the nearest hardware store and talked the owner into extending him some eight dollars' worth of credit so he could obtain the ingredients he needed to mix the formula. He hurried back to his room on which he owed the seven weeks' rent, and put the chemicals together. Then he sat down to let the power within tell him where to go to sell his product and himself.

The name W. & J. Sloane, a big Fifth Avenue furniture store, came to mind. This company obviously had an extensive leather upholstered furniture department. Mattern phoned and got the man in charge on the wire. He said: "I'm H. C. Mattern. I've developed a solution for cleaning and preserving all leather goods, especially leather furniture. I'd like to come up and demonstrate it for you."

"Come ahead," the executive invited. "If you've got something like that, we could certainly use it!"

When Mattern arrived with his solution, he was escorted to a storeroom and shown a leather upholstered divan in a sad state of disrepair. The leather was dried and cracked and soiled. It looked like a hopeless job, and the severest kind of a test for this chemical formula. But Mattern accepted the challenge. After one hour of hard, hard work, he called the executive back to look at the result. What that executive saw caused him to gasp in amazement, in utter disbelief.

"It looks as if you've substituted a new divan for me," he said. "This can't be the old one! Why, the cracks are softened up and smoothed out, the leather is pliable and alive again, and the soiled spots are all gone. Mr. Mattern —you've just earned yourself a contract to clean and preserve all of our leather upholstered furniture."

H. C. Mattern left the W. & J. Sloane company that morning with a check for $400.00, advance payment for the work he was to do for them.

"That something," the creative power you are going to learn how to operate for you, had done it! It would have rendered Mattern the same service years before, had he only called upon it, in the right way.

49

And what did Mattern do, in an effort to return thanks to God for the release of this power in and through him? He took a vow, that night, that he would never pass by another human being who needed help, that he would always take time to counsel with these persons, whoever they might be.

Don't read a book—study it!

Today, H. C. and his wife, Mary Mattern, are widely known from coast to coast, as the champion do-gooders of the country. They have given away thousands of copies of self-help books, which they have placed in the hands of bank presidents, leading industrialists and businessmen, congressmen, senators, governors, waitresses, porters, laborers, farmers, hotel clerks and maids, newsboys, housewives, people of all races, classes, professions and colors.

In the front of each book the Matterns write: "Do not read this book—*study* it!" Then they underline different paragraphs throughout with three different colored pencils, for emphasis. To make certain that the contents are studied, they staple the pages of different chapters or parts of chapters together, with the written instruction: "Do not remove these staples until you are sure you understand and practice what has gone before." Or: "Do not study this section for a month. It will take you that long to digest what you are now studying."

Mattern states that it takes them on the average an hour to fix each book, but "It's worth it—it makes all the difference in the world in what the individual gets from any book. Most people have the habit of reading, not studying, and they don't apply themselves. That's why they don't get anywhere."

Concerning the problems that various human beings are up against, Mattern declares: "Their problems are all fundamentally the same and can be solved only by calling upon the creative power within."

As for H. C. Mattern and his equally dynamic helpmate, Mary, their "Keep Smiling Always" salutation radiates constantly from them, and their indomitable spirit is best expressed by the slogan on their business card:

DOING THE IMPOSSIBLE—BECAUSE
WE KNOW HOW!

Well, what do you think of the creative power now? Are you getting ready to accept its operation in your life? If you are, you'd better start using Mattern's method, and underline every statement in this book that hits you between the eyes, that you feel can mean something special to you, so each thought will be hammered into your consciousness, and made a part of your thinking.

But, first, before you can release this power, you will have to rid your mind of a lot of wrong thoughts and feelings. This may be somewhat painful in the doing but it'll pay you tremendous dividends! Are you game? Can you face yourself? All right—let's go!

4

STOP—THINK—
AND ANALYZE YOURSELF!

A man's true greatness lies in the consciousness of an honest purpose in life, founded on a just estimate of himself and everything else, on frequent self-examinations, and a steady obedience to the rule which he knows to be right, without troubling himself about what others may think or say, or whether they do or do not do that which he thinks and says and does.

MARCUS AURELIUS

I take it there isn't an intelligent man or woman who isn't really interested in getting ahead, but I have often wondered if there isn't a negative quality or some inertia in most of us which precludes us from getting started.

I repeat an old story:

> Down on a levee in Mississippi, two Negroes were dozing. One of them yawned, stretched his arms and sighed:
> "Gee, I wish I had a million watermelons."
> The other Negro asked:
> "Rastus, if you had a million watermelons, would you give me half of them?"
> "No, sir!"
> "Would you give me a quarter of them?"
> "No, I wouldn't give you a quarter of them."
> "Rastus, if you had a million watermelons, wouldn't you give me even ten of them?"
> "No, sir! I wouldn't give you ten of them."
> "Well, wouldn't you give me one lousy watermelon?"
> "Say, Sam, I wouldn't give you even a bite of one if I had a million watermelons."
> "Why not, Rastus?"
> "Because you're too lazy to wish for yourself!"

There's much to be gleaned from that story. You'll understand as I proceed.

I am fully cognizant that some will scoff. There have always been scoffers, but scoffers never succeed. They never get any place in life, but simply become envious, while the doer or the person who is moving forward has to jump over or go around them. They have nothing but a nuisance value in life. Some of you may dismiss all of this as you have done before—as you always will—but for those of you who are interested, are still willing to learn, I promise you can learn and make progress for yourself.

It is easier to go with the current than fight against

it, but you must harmonize with others, with everything around you.

In the words of a great philosopher:

"No longer let thy breathing only act in concert with the air which surrounds thee, but let thy intelligence also now be in harmony with the intelligence which embraces all things."

It requires little effort to breathe but it does require the expenditure of energy to think. It shouldn't be necessary for me to explain further that I am suggesting that you put yourself in tune with the very stream of life itself. You who understand will appreciate that nature provides ways and means for all things to grow rightly.

Meditate for a moment and you'll realize I am giving truths which many may have forgotten. *There's the great fundamental law of compensation which makes all things right.*

There's no set rule for doing anything, because some of us perform one way and some another, just as two people might go across the river . . . one goes by one bridge and one by another . . . but they both ultimately get to their destination. In other words, after all is said and done, it's *results* that count, and, if you will make up your mind to exactly what you want and follow the simple rules which are given herein, everything you are after will be yours.

The time has come for you to stop and think and analyze yourself!

Just *what* do you believe about yourself—and *why?*

Do you believe you are getting out of life what you should? Do you believe you are giving to life what you should? Life, you know, is not a one-way street. It's a gift

to you from God, the Great Creator. But from the
ment you are born, you are basically on your own. You
have to draw the first breath to live—and you have to
keep on breathing, if you wish to remain on earth. You
have to take reasonable care of your body or you will suffer some form of ill health. You have to use your head
and what is inside it for something more than a hatrack.
If you don't, you won't get very far with either your mind
or your body.

The condition you are in right now largely depends
upon what you have been thinking and doing to and for
yourself—all your life. Nothing just happened to you by
accident. You are the sum total of all the causes and effects you have set up in yourself through your mental and
emotional attitudes. Their *end result* is the you that you
are right this minute!

Take a look in the mirror. Study every physical
movement. It tells a story. Each move you make marks
your personality, in outer expression.

Examine that look on your face: it indicates the way
you think. Your eyes—how do they appear to you? Are
they clear, steady and direct? The person you see in the
mirror is the one the other person sees. What kind of an
impression do you wish to make on him? That's entirely
up to you.

You know whether or not you have personality. If it
is absent or undeveloped, make up your mind to get it.
You can and you will, when you make up your mind and
do as suggested herein.

What *is* personality? What is it, when you get in the
presence of another person who has personality, that

grips you? What is it that causes you to *feel* his very presence—that overshadows you?

It's nothing more than a dynamic force coupled with will power which he is drawing from that huge reservoir of the subconscious. There are millions of people who have this personality (some say it's natural with them, and perhaps it is, but they are unconsciously using this power). It has been thrust upon them, or they have developed it without realizing, early in life, and when that thing called personality is backed up with will power, things move.

The appealing personality belongs to that man or woman who possesses self-confidence, self-assurance. These are people with a purpose; they know where they are going and how to get there; and this intensity of purpose shows in their faces. They have poise. They attract others to them as a magnet attracts iron filings. Everyone just groups around a radiant personality.

When you get to know yourself, you can develop this same intensity of purpose, this determination to get ahead. And, shortly, this determination will show in your eyes, your speech, your actions.

You have heard people say that a certain person has a penetrating gaze, that he looks right through one. What is it? Nothing more than that fire from within—intensity —or whatever you wish to call it, which means that the person who has that gaze usually gets what he wants. He compels, commands, attracts.

Remember, the eyes are the windows of the soul. Look at the photographs of successful men. Study their eyes and you will find that every one of them has that intensity. Therefore, I say, let it be reflected i... walk, in the way you carry yourself, and it long before people will feel your presence whe... through a crowd—and an individual prospect ...eel that personality when you talk with him.

To my way of thinking, selling bonds, books, clothes, insurance, electric service, washing machines, is no different from selling any other commodity . . . selling yourself or selling ideas. I have found that in trying to put over an idea, first I have had to believe in myself, then in the idea and my ability to sell both myself *and* the idea! I have also found that you have got to know what you are talking about and only hard, personal, persistent, intelligent study will enable you to do this.

How much do you know about yourself, about others, and the world you live in? The kind of personality you are expressing depends upon this knowledge. You can't express yourself with ease and assurance and authority unless you possess an awareness of self, of others and of the world!

Awaken! Know what is going on about you!
Get understanding!

You can develop and expand your personality by keeping step with the world's affairs. Keep informed. Find out all you can that is of interest about the people you have met or are to meet, so you'll have much more in common to talk about. You never know what a new friend or prospect may be interested in, and it's sometimes necessary to get his attention or your "break" through entirely irrelevant subjects. You can't always start a conversation about the weather or your aches and pains. Read the newspapers, current periodicals, listen to important radio newscasts and television commentators. Use your eyes and ears. Be sure you're up-to-date. I don't mean to cover every detail of a murder or a suicide, but get a digest of the day's activities, at home and abroad. It will enlarge your perspective.

Never forget—knowledge is power! That may sound like an old bromide, but, brother, it's true!

Who wants to listen to an uninformed, ignorant, self-centered individual?

Increase your knowledge, and the scope of your activities and interests will be greatly increased, as will the desire for greater things—larger things. As your desire expands, the things which you previously thought you wanted will become to your mind trivial and will be disregarded, which is another way of saying that you ultimately will hitch your wagon to a star and, when you do, you'll move with lightning-like speed!

Study, learn and work. Develop a keenness of observation. Step on the gas. Do better than that: get jet propulsion. Become alive for yourself, and you'll pass on this aliveness to the other fellow. You'll pep him up just by your being in his presence. Some of your magnetism will rub off on him and he will like you for it. You've heard people say: "I get a big kick out of being with so-and-so. He always gives me a lift!"

Get confidence, enthusiasm, let loose some of that inner fire—"that something"—and you'll set up like vibrations all around you. That's the theory of all life, as old as the world itself. Like begets like—tap, tap, tap! I'm repeating that statement, and I don't care how many times you've heard it before. Perhaps if I repeat it often enough—tap, tap, tap!—you'll never forget it. Like begets like. A laugh brings a laugh, a good deed calls for a good deed, riches beget riches, love, love—you go on from there! It works! It's contagious! The old law of attraction never fails.

But don't get the idea that I am giving you an over-size wishbone and all you have to do is sit down and start talking to yourself, and by using repetition, get what you want. It's not that easy! You've got to have the *wish*bone backed up with a *back*bone. And that isn't all. The *wish*bone and the *back*bone must be coordinated and synchronized to a point where they are operating in perfect harmony. When they are in tune, you will find personality developing. Then put action, energy into your scheme and everything will move before you.

I take it that all of us have admired that intense type of person. I mean by that, one whose shoulders are back, whose chest is out, whose head is up and whose eyes are alert. It is easy to pick out in any organization those whose feet lag, whose shoulders droop, whose chins sag and whose eyes are a blank. Drifters, loafers, quitters.

Discover your faults

First, measure yourself. Then study those with whom you are associated, and you can tell, at almost a glance, those who will make progress and those doomed to failure.

Are you close to that category? If you are, snap out of it!

The fault, dear Brutus, is not in our stars,
But in ourselves, that we are underlings.

William Shakespeare wrote that, as you know, and it's plain to be seen, in his writings, that he knew and used this inner power in his life. He rose high above the commonplace and won for himself an immortal niche in the literary hall of fame, through reliance upon the creative power within.

Yes, the fault is in yourself, if you are not what you want to be and where you want to be.

If you are timid, backward, in a rut and an underling, it is because of yourself. Blame not the stars. Blame not society. Blame not the world. Blame *yourself*. Again I say, change gears. Get out of low and shift into high. Start picturing what you really want to be and you'll start to move.

Take warning that thought can operate in reverse. You can go backward through wrong thinking just as fast as you can go forward through right thinking.

This kind of "reverse thinking" has brought on depressions, and can bring on depressions again. If the mind of man becomes panicky, if enough individuals become obsessed with fear and greed, if the psychology of scarcity sweeps through the land, if great numbers of people become too demanding or move too strongly in a certain direction, stock markets can become upset and the economy of the world can be affected.

You know, when you are depressed you tend to depress those around you. When the barometer falls, it's a sign of storm conditions. A turned-down mouth has led to many turndowns. Don't carry your griefs and troubles around with you. No one wants to share them. People have griefs and troubles enough of their own.

Stop your moping!

Picture yourself wrapping up your griefs and troubles in a nice little neat bundle and leaving them by the roadside. Better yet, see yourself dropping them off a bridge so they'll float away on the stream and never come back again.

You say, "But it can't be done!" and I answer, "Is it helping you solve your problems and your heartaches, letting them weigh you down in mind and body all the time?"

Get out from under! You can't be yourself, it is impossible to make the right impression on others, to attract good things to you, when you are staggering under a load of things that have already happened, which can no longer be helped and which cannot be cured by moping about.

If worry had the power to solve a problem, I would worry twenty-four hours a day, and I'd ask you to help me. But worry, unhappily, only multiplies your troubles.

Line up all the chronic worriers in the world, and they would reach almost to the moon and back. You've seen many men and women who look as if they were going to cloud up and rain any minute. They belong to the Loyal Order of Sad Sacks and Crepe-Hangers. Everything that happens to them is bad or going to be bad. They've temporarily lost the capacity to see good in anything.

They can't enjoy the present because they are bemoaning the past and afraid of the future.

One of the wisest men I ever knew, a man high in mental and spiritual development, said to me: "Never for one moment forget this: *life is an individual proposition.* No matter how much you may wish, at times, to shift responsibility for your thoughts and acts to others, or to escape from the consequences of certain experiences in which you have become involved, you are living in a world of cause and effect—a world in which nothing actually happens by accident—and you, yourself, set up the causes by your own thinking, good or bad, for the things that happen to you!"

I have proved this, time and again, in my own life, and so have you, if you will only admit it to yourself. But when I've made this statement to some men and women, they've said to me: "That's a frightening thought. Do you mean that I have attracted failure, economic need, ill health, dislike, loss of friends, unhappiness . . . ?" And when I have told such people: "Yes, if any of these conditions have come upon you, you have your own self to blame," they said, "But we didn't *picture* these things!"

No, perhaps they didn't—directly. They didn't *see* themselves failing, running short of funds, suffering a nervous breakdown, growing unpopular, losing friends, ending up unhappy. But their mental attitudes were expressed in this kind of thoughts:

"Wouldn't you just know this would happen to me?"

"There's no use trying—I just can't do it!"

"I don't want to meet him or her. . . . I know I won't like them!"

"It's just my luck to have this happen. I'm always getting the worst of it."

"Oh, I feel so bad, I wish I could die."

"I'm going broke—there's no way out."

"Yes, I'm feeling fairly well today—but this doesn't mean anything. I'll probably feel worse tomorrow!"

Aren't these wonderful suggestions? Can you possibly picture, with the knowledge of mind you have now gained, how *any* of these thoughts could attract good?

On the contrary, this kind of thinking can only bring one result. Yet, many of us, carelessly, in moments of emotional depression, give voice to such thoughts and then wonder why so many things go wrong in our lives.

Prepare yourself to face anything!

So: take stock of yourself! We are living, as you know, in a terrific age—an amazing age. To many whose minds are unprepared, it is a bewildering, frightening age.

The tempo of life and developments is increasing at a rapid rate. Things are unfolding almost too fast for the mind of man to grasp. More and more earth-shaking developments are on the way. Much that was considered impossible a few years ago has already been accomplished. Anything may happen from now on—and probably will!

You must train yourself to be mentally alert, to maintain an open mind, to make contact with your cre-

63

ative power within, so you can adapt yourself to the changes that are coming; so you will have the insight, the understanding and the courage to meet them.

You must learn how to perceive the truth—to accept what appeals to your past experience, your reason and your intuition—and to reserve judgment on all things with which you are unfamiliar, until you can prove them out or test them in your own life.

It is not enough for you to learn the laws of mind. You must learn how to *use* your mind in accordance with these laws.

You've heard the old, old adage: "Faith without works is dead." You must *work* with yourself if you would develop the creative power within, so it can do what it has done and is doing for others.

The fortunate men and women of the world are those who know how to visualize, how to eliminate their fears and worries, how to remain inwardly calm and poised, no matter what the circumstances, how to assume a positive mental attitude, and how to retain emotional stability under pressure.

This should be your great goal in life, to realize a like attainment. It will be your only guidance and protection in this fast-moving world of today.

Abandon all limited thinking!

Prepare your mind now by putting aside all narrow and limited thinking. Never say again that *anything* is impossible, no matter how impossible it may seem at the moment. Don't restrict and shackle your mind by small and prejudiced thinking. Free your consciousness of feelings of resentment, antagonism, hate and like emotional reactions toward others. This kind of thoughts is keeping you from thinking straight, from getting the right perspective toward others and yourself. They are holding you back from progress, preventing your creative power from working through you.

You can overcome the effects that wrong thinking has had upon you. But to do this, you must gain emotional control; you must learn how to relax your physical body, how to make your conscious mind passive, and how to place the right pictures of what you desire in mind. You must learn how to release the hold that past mistakes, now stored in consciousness, have upon you.

Since like attracts like (tap, tap, tap—I'm repeating this again!), good attracts good and bad attracts bad. It's as simple as that, but you can't straighten yourself out, without facing your past.

Men and women say to me, "But I'm trying to *forget* my past!"

Alas, the mind doesn't operate that way. What it takes into consciousness, it hangs onto, unless you, through an act of recognition, resolution and will, *change* the picture—or let go of it!

How often do you let yourself be upset about something someone does or says? You store the picture of each incident and feeling in mind.

When you think of this person, you call up the same feelings against him, until you have overcome them. If you don't change them, they exist as irritations in consciousness. Irritations eventually find their reflection in some disturbed body condition or illness, or an unhappy human experience.

Do you want to permit these past irritations to attract similar disturbances in your future? Then get busy and eliminate them from your consciousness.

Stop kidding yourself!

You will have to do your own analyzing. You know yourself better than any close friend or relative can ever know you. You may have been able to mask your real feelings and thoughts from others; but you can tell, deep down within, what you really think and feel about anything or anybody. If these thoughts and feelings are not good, get busy and *make* them good!

Forgive others for what they've done to you. Assume your share of the blame. Don't hold resentments or grudges or hates. They are poisoning your mind and your body, upsetting the chemistry of your physical organism, making you susceptible to all manner of possible diseases and illnesses. Doctors now attribute such afflictions as arthritis, rheumatism, shingles, some forms of epilepsy and many other illnesses to nervous and emotional disturbances. It has even been found that many who have cancer can retard its progress if they can control their emotions and maintain an optimistic, fearless attitude toward it.

"That something" in mind has unlimited power—to overcome, to heal, to create, to attract—once you learn how to use it.

The development of this power is up to you. Are

66

you willing to put forth the effort? If you are, go with me, from chapter to chapter, studying and applying . . . studying and applying . . . and when we reach the end of this journey together—you will have the answer to your problems, and will be on your successful, happy way—*alone*.

5

HOW TO CREATE
MIND PICTURES

Look within. Within is the foun-
tain of good, and it will ever
bubble up, if thou wilt ever dig.

AN ANCIENT SAYING

Before you can really reach and control and direct "that something," you need to know just how your mind functions. This creative power is the most important part of your mind, but it is elusive and intangible and difficult to contact, consciously, until you have gained an understanding of your inner consciousness.

Did you know, for instance, that you actually do not think in words . . . you think in pictures! And, because you think in pictures, and *not* in words, your mind, in its "mechanical" functioning, operates no differently from that of Primitive Man, who lived thousands of years ago.

He, too, thought in pictures, before language was

evolved. When he was gone from his cave home, on the hunt, and returned to his tribe, the only way he could convey to them what had happened to him was to draw crude pictures in charcoal or chisel them on the stone walls of his cave.

Gradually, as primitive man drew pictures of similar experiences over and over again, and associated sounds with certain objects and happenings, he had only to start a familiar picture and onlookers knew instantly what he meant. These early pictures eventually reduced themselves to symbols, the symbols grouped together became letters, then words, and finally sentences . . . and first language was born.

But with all our vaunted civilization of today, with all the languages that have evolved, with the enormous vocabulary of words that modern man possesses to describe his feelings and ideas and the world about him, he still thinks basically in mental pictures. I can easily prove this to you.

Take your time, and think of some little unusual experience you have had this day. As you recall it to mind, you see, in your mind's eye, pictures of your doing something, being somewhere, meeting someone—whatever the incident may have been. But, you are powerless to convey to me what happened to you until you grope for words, the symbols of this happening, so you can tell me about it. I, in turn, as I listen to your words, have to translate these words into pictures in my own mind's eye, in order to see and comprehend what you experienced.

So it is clearly evident that you think basically, as I have said, in pictures. This is one of the most important facts you can ever learn about your mind. And the next important fact is this: what you picture in your mind, if it unites with the creative power within, can attract to you whatever you fear or desire.

The creative power is like a magnet

This is true because this creative power operates like a magnet. Give it a strong, clear picture of what you want and this creative power starts to work magnetizing conditions about you—attracting to you the things, resources, opportunities, circumstances and even the people you need, to help bring to pass in your outer life what you have pictured!

You don't believe it? Think back over your life! Recall the times you lived in fear something would happen and eventually it came to pass. You perhaps didn't realize it—but those fear pictures had so impressed "that something" within that you caused it to attract wrong conditions to you and made you susceptible to the very thing you feared.

You see, this creative power within doesn't reason. It just produces for you what you order in the form of a mental picture, with strong feelings of fear or desire behind it. That's why that inner power is TNT, either for or against you, depending on whether your thinking is constructive or destructive.

Now you can understand how certain good, as well as bad, things have happened throughout your life. "That something" has been serving you, and the kind of results you have obtained has depended on the kind of mental pictures you have presented to it.

How does your life add up on this basis? Has it

been filled, thus far, with about as many unhappy experiences as happy ones? If so, you'll want to change that in a hurry! And you can change it, at once, by a fundamental change in your mental attitude, by overcoming your fears and worries and replacing them with positive, confident, courageous thinking.

There is no longer any doubt about it (and there never has been to those who have understood the operation of consciousness) that "as you *picture* in your mind and heart, so are you!"

Keep this great fact always before you. Let it dominate your every-day thinking. Check yourself each time you tend to become disturbed, mentally and emotionally, and to store unhappy, destructive mental pictures in your mind. Do you want to pass on such pictures for your creative power to work upon? Do you wish these fears or desires to be magnetized so that they attract similar experiences to you? If not, let go of this kind of pictures at once. Change them for the better. Drop all feelings of fear or resentment or hate or jealousy—whatever these feelings may be—and substitute the right kind of feelings and mental attitudes. The moment you do so, you destroy the power these wrong pictures would eventually have over you.

Beware of the wrong use of TNT!

TNT is wonderful when you use it right—but it can "mow you down" if you set up the wrong charge in yourself.

Once you have cleared your mind of wrong mental pictures and emotional reactions, you are ready to picture, with faith and confidence, the achievement of good things.

Faith is the energizer of the creative power, "that something" within. I'll have more to say about that later, but you must believe that what you picture can come to pass. Doubt will destroy your picture and demagnetize the creative power so that you will get a half-result or no result at all, or even a wrong result.

Picture whatever you desire as though it has already been achieved in mind. See yourself *having* something, *being* something, or *doing* something as an accomplished fact. Don't try to picture the individual steps that you think you should take to get where you want to go. Your conscious mind is so limited in its operation—limited by your five physical senses—that it cannot know what is the best move for you to make or the best direction to take. But your subconscious mind, "that something" within, is not limited by time or space. It can function on all levels and in all directions at once, and put you in touch with all manner of opportunities and people that you do not even know of, consciously, as yet.

Whatever you need to fit into the pattern of achievement that you have pictured, will be attracted to you by the power within if you persist in your visualizing, day after day, and put forth every effort in support of your heartfelt desire.

This is the simple technique to follow. It will produce infallible results, in due course of time, if you master the art of *picturization*.

But I should make clear that there are two types of minds, the *visualizing* type and the *feeling* type! If you find it difficult to create a picture in your mind's eye of what you want in life, don't strain in an attempt to do it. You are probably the *feeling* type . . . and all you then have to do is to concentrate on an imaginary focal point in the dark room of your inner mind and let yourself *feel* that what you desire has been accomplished in consciousness—that all that remains is for it to be materialized by the magnetic creative power in your outer world. You will get the same results as those who find it easy to visualize.

You must know how to relax!

Of course, it should go without saying that before you can concentrate upon what you desire, you have to know how to relax your physical body and make your conscious mind passive.

Can you relax? Can you let go of your body with your mind so that it loses all tenseness, so that you can become "un-self-conscious" of your body while you are meditating or visualizing?

Many men and women have told me that they have great difficulty becoming "still" in body and in mind. They feel a tightness in the back of the neck, across the eyes, in the solar plexus—in one or all of these places. They say they hadn't realized how tense and nervous they really are until they had tried to become quiet, physically and mentally. Some tell me that their conscious mind is filled with all sorts of fragmentary fears and worries and jumbled thoughts, that they just can't make it a blank and get ready to picture what they really want.

Well, I don't wonder. So many of us live such hectic every-day lives. We've formed such bad habits in our thinking, and few of us have attained any dependable emotional control. All sorts of little things upset us and we carry these upsets around with us all day. They are still with us at night when we try to relax and do some constructive thinking for a change. The result is that when we do quiet down, we are even more conscious of the disturbances of the day which dramatize themselves in the forefront of our minds.

How can we get rid of them? That's a $64.00 question! It's worth a lot more than that to you, if you can get the answer. You've *got* to get the answer if you are ever to picture clearly and confidently your objectives in mind.

Have you ever heard that it is impossible to have any more than one thought in your conscious mind at one time? It's true! At any given moment, you can be conscious of but *one* thought. The secret of concentration is fixing the attention of the conscious mind upon an imagined focal point in consciousness—such as a mental screen. Visualize that screen as stretched across the dark room of your inner mind, and as long as you hold your attention on it, other stray thoughts and fears and worries can't chase across that screen.

Project your own picture!

Take your time, quietly, relaxedly, and throw your own mental picture on that screen. Don't try to hold it too long. The instant you feel that the creative power

74

within has received this picture, say to yourself, "It is finished . . . it has been created"—whatever you feel like saying which adds conviction to your visualization or your feelings, and let go.

If you took a picture with a camera, you wouldn't keep opening up the camera and looking at the negative to see if the picture was developed, would you? Have faith that the creative power—"that something" within—will do the developing for you. Go about your life activities with the happy expectation that what you have pictured is in the process of materialization. But repeat the picturization every day, several times a day, and at night before retiring, until what you have pictured or felt yourself having achieved in mind has become a fact in real life.

Now, the question is, how do you go to work to help make what you have pictured come true? You can't just sit around, expecting this creative power to do the whole job for you. The best way to prove to the creative power within that you mean business is to go to work on your own and do everything you can toward the reaching of your objective. Sometimes you won't reach the objective you think you are aiming at—but will accomplish something even better.

Bill McDaniel was one of New York City's finest insurance salesmen. He believed in the higher powers of mind and attributed his success to his developed use of them. He operated in the absolute faith that when he pictured a sale of a policy or an annuity as accomplished in mind, it was all but wrapped up. However, he didn't indulge in any wishful thinking or pollyannish affirmations. He did plenty of leg work, made the personal contacts and set the stage for the consummation of each deal. There were times when his intuition told him he shouldn't press, that he should sit tight and wait till he had the hunch to move in for the kill.

One of these times was when he had been trying to sell a Wall Street broker a fifty-thousand-dollar annuity. This man had been a hard nut to crack. He had one idiosyncrasy well known to his business associates. He was a crank on punctuality. When he made an appointment with a man, if this man was so much as five minutes late, he wouldn't see him. He had a great sense of his own importance and the value of time. Because he was out of the city a great deal, it was even difficult to make a date with him.

This particular morning, Bill McDaniel was lucky. He had given his man a ring and the prospect said he would see him at eleven A.M. sharp. Bill took the subway, allowing himself plenty of leeway to get to his appointment on time. At Times Square he had to change trains for Wall Street, and as he was hurrying through the crowd, he passed a little old lady of foreign extraction, who was clutching an old-fashioned handbag, and sobbing from fright and bewilderment. No one was paying any attention to her. She was just one of the many minor tragedies that occur practically unnoticed any day in a big city like New York. But the mental image of this pathetic old woman stuck in Bill's mind as he ran down the subway steps toward his train which was pulling in. He glanced at his wrist watch. It was twenty minutes to eleven. There would be another train along in a few minutes. He could still make it. Bill turned about, ran back up the steps and approached the little old woman.

"Hello, Mother," he greeted her. "What's the matter? You lost?"

She looked up at him, hopefully. "Yah," she said.

"What's your name, Mother—where do you live?" asked Bill.

She shook her head. "I don't know."

"Do you have any relatives—a son or daughter?"

"I don't know!" she said, piteously.

The poor woman was so upset and dazed she couldn't think.

"Mother," said Bill, "do you mind if I look in your pocketbook?"

He took hold of it and she handed it to him. Bill opened the tattered handbag and rummaged among its assortment of odds and ends. He came across a piece of paper with an address scribbled on it. There was a woman's name and a street number in Brooklyn.

Bill read this to the little old woman and asked: "Is this your daughter?"

"Yah, yah!" said the woman, her face lighting up. "My daughter!"

"Is that where you're going?" asked Bill.

"Yah, yah!"

Bill took her by the arm. "Come with me, Mother. Don't worry. Everything's going to be all right. I'll put you on the right train."

He led her down the stairs. A train to Brooklyn was just about to pull out. Bill waved at the guard on the nearest car.

"Hold it!" he cried. "This woman's lost. I've her address here. She's trying to get to her daughter in Brooklyn. Will you see that she gets off at the right stop and have the station master put her in a cab or phone her daughter, so she can come and get her?"

"Sure will, Mister!" said the guard, taking the slip of paper with the address. "Step in, Mother. We'll take care of you!"

Bill saw the little old woman safely on the train. She turned, as the door was closing on her and said in a broken voice, filled with gratitude: "God bless you!"

How opportunity sometimes knocks!

Then Bill glanced again at his wrist watch. Seven minutes to eleven. He had missed his appointment. No use going on down to Wall Street. His prospect wouldn't see him. If it had been almost anyone else but Bill he would have said: "That's what I get for being a Good Samaritan . . . lost a chance to sell a fifty-thousand-dollar annuity." He confessed to having felt a stab of bitter disappointment. He had planned on making this contact for weeks, and it was hard to understand why he had been waylaid. No doubt someone else would eventually have come to this old lady's rescue, someone who hadn't been so pressed for time. But for some reason he couldn't figure out, he just hadn't been able to continue on his way without doing what he could for her. Perhaps it was because the thought had occurred to him, "That's someone's mother. If it were my mother, wouldn't I appreciate any help that might be extended to her?"

Oh, well, it was all over now—and he was glad he had

done what he did. He would always have been haunted by that appealing look she had cast at him as he passed, that desperate, poignant reaching out for human aid . . . if he had gone on about his business. Still, you didn't line up good prospects like this man every day. . . .

As he was about to board a subway train for his up-town office, it suddenly occurred to Bill that he was in the vicinity of Fifth Avenue and Forty-Second Street, the business address of another prospect, with whom he had left the figures on a hundred-thousand annuity six weeks before. This man had been in Europe and Bill had read in the papers that he had recently returned. Wouldn't hurt, since he was so near, to drop in on the chance of saying "hello."

The prospect's reception room was jammed with people waiting to see him and Bill turned away. He didn't have an appointment, and it wouldn't do him any good to wait, with a line-up like that ahead of him. But as he stepped toward the elevator, he noticed that the man's private office door was open into the corridor. It was a hot August day and he apparently needed cross-ventilation.

Acting on impulse, Bill walked down the hall and looked in. To his amazement, the man was seated in his office alone, studying some papers on his desk. He looked up and both men saw each other at the same moment.

"Bill McDaniel!" exclaimed the man. "Come on in! . . . This *is* a coincidence! I was just going to phone you! I've been studying your annuity proposition. I was in a car accident last night and I decided I'd like to have some more coverage."

79

"But you've got an office full of people!" said Bill.

"Let them wait," said the man, "this is more important."

Forty minutes later, Bill McDaniel walked out with a hundred-thousand-dollar annuity sale under his belt. Had it not been for this little old lady. . . . Yes, you get the point. . . .

"That taught me one of the biggest lessons of my life," Bill said to me, as he related this experience. " 'Cast your bread upon the waters'—and it comes back *cake!*"

There is a lesson in this for you. Visualize, as best you can, what you desire; do your darndest to help bring what you are picturing to pass through your own efforts, when things seemingly go bad have faith that they will lead to something just as good or better—and they often will!

Thought, contacting "that something," brings everything, with nature's exceptions, into manifestation. A single thought not followed up—a flash dismissed or lost—may be compared to a bobbing cork, aimless and without purpose. However, the *same* thought, the picture of the thing you want, kept constant, will attract its object, just as a magnet attracts. The larger and more powerful the magnet, the greater its drawing force, and so it is with sustained thought. The more powerful it becomes the more it attracts.

Just as a huge magnifying glass drawing the sun's rays and kept focused on a certain spot will burn a hole, so will powerful sustained thought (the vivid mental picture) directed to or on its object correlate. However, you must mentally see the picture of your object or ideal as a reality ... see every detail of the picture as being in existence just as you want the object or ideal actually to be ... then, as if by magic, the chain will link itself together.

Now go back and reread this again until it is permanently impressed upon you.

6

HOW "PIPE DREAMS"
CAN BECOME REALITIES

There is an oft-repeated phrase with which you must be familiar. It is, "I can dream, can't I?" But this exclamation usually has the tone of futility in it, as though the person making it had no faith that his dreams will come true.

Actually, he who dares dream and believe in his dreams is the creator, to a great extent, of his future.

You would not be a normal, average human being if you did not have hidden desires and so-called "pipe dreams." While you may not confess them to anyone, you do build air castles on occasion, seeing yourself doing something or going somewhere or having something—and you take a certain joy just imagining, for the moment, that these air castles are real. It's seldom, however, that you put the power of your own feeling and conviction behind your dreams. You've never had the faith that they could be converted into actual happenings, if you took them seriously instead of fancifully.

"Oh, I never expect to do anything like this," a woman said to me once, who had been day-dreaming about a trip to Europe. "But it's fun to imagine doing it, anyway."

When I assured her that she could go to Europe if she really wanted to do so, she laughed and said: "I don't see how. I'd never have money enough to do that!"

"You certainly won't as long as you continue that negative thinking," I pointed out. "Every other statement you make about yourself is 'I never expect . . . I never will have . . .' and so on. What you are doing is instructing the creative power within not to do anything for you—to keep you from having enough money to do things—and you are getting just what you are picturing."

It took her a little while to get onto what she was doing to herself. Then she said: "All right. From now on I'm going to think positive thoughts. But I still can't see how I'm ever going to get to Europe."

"Leave that to your subconscious—to the power within," I advised. "Just picture yourself making the trip to Europe and let the creative power work out the way you are going to get to go—and the means!"

"It sounds pretty screwy to me," she said, "but I'll try it."

"You've got to have faith," I warned. "You just can't go through the motions of picturing yourself in Europe, without faith, and ever get there."

"Okay! I'll give it everything I've got!" she said. "And we'll see what happens."

"Hold on—you're expressing doubt," said I. "You're not going to see *what* happens—you're going to see *it* happen!"

83

"I'll never get the hang of this kind of thinking," she laughed.

Eight months later I received a letter from this woman—from Europe—but I didn't recognize her by name, until she identified herself.

"I'm here," she reported. "It worked, just as you said it would. Only I had to get married to do it!"

How wonderful, thought I, "that something" within brought her not only a trip to Europe, but a husband, too! When you start picturing good things coming your way, you may get more than you bargain for!

Start your mind pumping!

Clarence Saunders, now 67, is on his way to his third fortune. Before he was 35, he had his first fortune. His colossal "pipe dream" of the famous Piggly Wiggly super market chain had paid off. Saunders maintains it's easy to think "million-dollar ideas" once you gear your mind to it. "My mind is pumping all the time," he declares, "and I can never tell what the pump is going to bring up —but I just give the creative power free rein and it comes up with something of value, time after time." To-day, Saunders is launching his new chain grocery idea which he calls the "Foodelectric." The store operates so automatically that the customer can collect her groceries herself, wrap them and act as her own cashier. "It eliminates the check-out crush, cuts overhead expenses and enables a small staff to handle a tremendous volume," says Saunders. "I can handle a $2,000,000 volume a year with only eight employees, whereas any other supermarket of the same size would employ at least forty, perhaps sixty-five people. I've made and lost millions in my life—but I'm on my way to my next million now!"

How can you stop a man like that? Is your mind functioning on all cylinders at 67? Or will it be? It won't, unless you've trained it to operate. You are carrying a potential fortune around in your head at all times. "Start your mind pumping," Saunders suggests, "and you may strike oil!"

"Pipe dreams," you say. "Nothing like this could ever happen to me." Watch that negative thinking! You can't conceive of the possibilities within you, once you give the creative power within an opportunity to be of service.

Did the Wright brothers have a "pipe dream" when they pictured themselves building and flying the first airplane? Many "unseeing" people thought so and heaped ridicule upon them, but this didn't stop the Wrights. They had the courage and the faith to keep on dreaming and working, in the face of skepticism, and brought a new mode of travel to the world.

So few of us have vision. We cannot see beyond the present moment. We become so immersed in our current difficulties and problems that we can visualize no way out.

"Pipe dreaming" is a way of escape into the future—a way of freeing yourself from the present and creating new opportunities and developments. I don't mean that you can sidestep present responsibilities and problems . . . but the cure for many of them lies in your future, as does your hope for self-betterment.

"Look forward—never backward," has been the admonition of wise men. They have known that the past

can do nothing for you, but the future always holds promise if, in the words of Peter Ibbetson, you "dream true."

How great is your faith?

How long could you persist in a dream, something
you very much wanted, if it took some years to come true?
Would your faith waver? Would your enthusiasm die
out? Would you decide that the apparent obstacles were
too many, that they could never be overcome? Would
you compromise with yourself, and settle for something
less than you had originally visualized?

Ask yourself these questions as I let Zora Adler, of
Glendale, California, tell of her pipe dream which she
carried in mind and heart for twenty-two years—and
which she and her husband, Dan, have just brought to
fruition! It is one of the most remarkable and inspiring
demonstrations of visualization and faith and never-
give-up spirit and harmony and co-operation, and the
perfect working of the power within, that has ever come
to my attention.

Here is Mrs. Adler's thrilling story in her own
words:

"I suppose my dream really started twenty-two years
ago when I would look up at the hills above our home in
Glendale and would say to Dan, my husband, 'Some day,
let's build a house up there.'

"We *did* build one, nine years later, half-way between there and my real objective. But I still had my
heart set on the heights. Some day we would have our
home where I had originally seen it. And, because I noticed that most people walk worriedly and look at the

ground, I decided that the answer to that was to take my two little girls for hikes into the hills where there were trees and clouds to make them look up. Somehow, there is so much to see when the chin and eyes are lifted.

"It was on such a hike into the hills that I walked out onto a plateau, overlooking the whole San Fernando Valley, on into Los Angeles, Long Beach and even Santa Monica Palisades—and I felt an immediate attachment for the location.

"Impulsively, ecstatically, I said to the girls: 'Let's build a house here!' They were very excited for, little as they were, they loved it, too! But, imagine my saying a thing like that—getting such an idea—when we had just completed a new home, scarcely three years before!

"Well, we hurried home fast, almost afraid the place might be gone before we could come back with their Daddy to show him this new location for a home. I didn't stop to think that he might be upset by such a show of interest in another building site—and wonder if his wife was the sort of woman who just never would be satisfied. But instead, to my surprise and delight, he went right back with us, and as soon as he saw the hilltop and the view, he said: 'Find out who owns it.' That was thirteen years ago!

"The next morning, I went to the City Hall in Glendale and found it was owned by a Mr. and Mrs. Jennings who lived in San Diego. I wrote the usual letter of inquiry and sent it on its way—holding the thought that the lot was for sale and that we could have it! Somehow, from the very beginning, I never doubted that the lot would be ours.

"I was not at all surprised when Mr. Jennings wrote

and told us we could buy it—but the miracle was yet to come. The price was over our heads since we were buying our present home and business, and with prospects of more children, we felt we should not take the big step. But every Sunday afternoon we would walk up to 'our lot' and draw house plans in the dirt.

"On such a Sunday, I was literally dancing around with the girls and my husband for I had hit on a perfect plan for the house and could just *see* it standing there all finished!

"An elderly couple had come up on the hill while we were there and I noticed they had been eyeing us. After a while they sauntered over to where we were preoccupied with our 'blueprint' in the dirt, and this was our conversation:

"*The Elderly Gentleman:* I see you are drawing house plans!

"*Mrs. Adler:* Oh, yes, we are going to build a house here!

"*The Elderly Gentleman:* Are you interested in this lot?

"*Mrs. Adler:* Yes, indeed—this is our lot and new home site!

"*The Elderly Gentleman* (laughingly): This is very interesting, for I am Mr. Jennings. Mrs. Jennings and I own this property!

"*Mrs. Adler* (a bit taken aback): Well, Mr. Jennings, it is very nice to meet you—but I am not going to take back a single word of it. We won't be building right away but I feel I should let you know that that is exactly what we are going to do. Since there are three other lots, won't you be our neighbors?

"Mr. Jennings smiled and replied that they would be delighted and would build on the front lot, about fifty feet below ours.

"Over the span of the next eleven years, Mr. Jennings wrote us three times, each time saying he was going to sell the lots and if we were still interested, to let him know right away. I always answered that we were interested but would have to wait. The 'time was not ripe for us'—but I did finally tell him to go right ahead and put the property on the market. I stated however that I thought it only fair to warn him, so he wouldn't be wasting his time, that the *Adlers* are the ones who will build on it, even if he should sell it, so it probably would be a useless bit of buying and selling to let it go to someone else meanwhile. We laughed about it—but he didn't really suspect how seriously I *meant* it!

"Almost eleven years passed by—and then I contacted Mr. Jennings again, saying we were now ready to buy the lot! He came to Glendale immediately and we signed the papers. What a glorious feeling it was—and such a fulfillment! As we rose to leave the office, Mr. Jennings took my hand and said:

"'Mrs. Adler—I think you put the jinx on me!'

"'Oh, no, Mr. Jennings—I wouldn't do that to anyone!'

"'Well, for your information, I think you should know that three separate times, we sat at a desk just like this to sell that lot to someone else—and something happened and the deals fell through! . . . You jinxed me, all right! All of the other lots sold and this—the best one of all—had apparently been reserved for *you!*'

"I could have told him that I had placed it all in

God's hands some thirteen, if not twenty-two, years before, and had known that our dream house was already a reality then!

You must have unwavering faith!

"But the end is not yet! After gaining actual ownership, at last, we contacted a building contractor. He looked at our plans and told us that unless we had $36,-000 in our pocket we could not possibly build that house. I laughed and asked him if he had ever known anyone with that much money? He replied that the thing wrong with people like us was that we had big ideas . . . that we should go to an architect and tell him how much money we had and then let him build a house accordingly. We told him that was not the house we wanted, and left. You see, I drew all the plans, too, and I wasn't settling for anything less than what had been visualized!

"Anyway, a bit dampened in spirit, I turned to my darling husband who said: 'Where's your faith? We'll build that house! There are other contractors. He just isn't the one to build it for us! Let's go and see Mr. Brown. He has a lot of information on these things.'

"We did—and Mr. Brown directed us to a possible solution. It all led to a contractor who had the exact set-up we needed. Our house is exactly as we planned it —every door and every nail—and it cost us thousands less than $36,000! All things are surely possible in God!

"Now that our dream house is practically finished and we are ready to move in, everyone who comes onto the property and sees the home which has had God as a co-builder, remarks that there is something very different about the feeling of the place. It is not just another house and lot. The craftsmen have all been most congenial and happy, there is an atmosphere of peace and contentment and harmony everywhere.

"It is interesting to note, too, that buying at the time we did was much the best. It was well worth waiting for; because, had we purchased the property previously, we would not have been protected on the utilities as we were later . . . we even got a sewer! And I might add, our lot was several, in fact three thousand, dollars less than the next selling price on a lot—and you know, after seeing it, how much more desirable our hilltop location is than any of the surrounding locations!

"We would be a pretty difficult family to convince that the best partner anyone could have is not God and the God Power within!"

What do you think of "pipe dreams" now? Like the O'Briens, the Adlers attained their "dream home." It took them years longer. They didn't find it ready-made. They found the location first, then created the house in their minds and drew blueprints of it, and held to the thought that they would be able to buy the site they wanted, and get the money, one day, to build this home. It required unwavering faith and persistence, never losing sight of their goal, never permitting themselves to be disturbed or to change their original pictures and desires, sticking to what they wanted—no matter what happened!

Was it worth it? You bet it was! And you'll say the same when you set your goal in life—whatever it is—and call upon this creative power within to serve you, as it has served and is serving the O'Briens and the Adlers of this world! This power never fails you . . . if you don't fail it!

The Adlers have brought up their daughters to think as they think, to picture happiness and success and good health for themselves, to be free of fear and worry thoughts, to add the power of their own visualization to the mental picturings of the parents. There is tremendous power generated in a family circle when all are in harmony. "Where two or more are gathered together"—things happen!

Breathe the breath of life into your "pipe dreams" by believing in them, by maintaining your faith and your dreams, unfalteringly, come what may, and eventually, if you persevere, what once was a dream will become a glorious reality!

7

TAP—TAP—TAP!

Let's set the stage. I want to call your attention to the powerful effect of repetition or reiteration.

For example, take a pneumatic chisel. You have seen one used in breaking up solid concrete or piercing holes through steel. It's the *tap, tap, tap, tap* of that chisel with a terrific force behind it, which causes disintegration of the particles and makes a dent or hole in the object on which it is placed.

All of us have heard of the old torture system of dripping water on the forehead. Perhaps you are familiar with Kipling's "Boots." It's the *tramp, tramp* of *boots, boots,* that makes men mad. It's the constant, never-ending repetition that penetrates.

While you may realize how repetition works on material things, you may not thoroughly appreciate the tremendous impression that repetition also makes upon the human mind.

But you've long since recognized that the fundamental of advertising is its repetition, its appeal by reiteration:

"It floats. . . ." "There's a reason. . . ." "I'd walk a mile. . . ." "They're kind to the throat. . . ." "Good-to-the-Last-Drop. . . ." And so on and so on, over and over.

They shout these slogans at you, sing them, play them, picture them—there's no escape—by constant repetition the advertised merits of each product are dinned into your consciousness until you almost spout slogans in your sleep. Tap-tap-tap—they beat in upon you every time you turn on your radio or television set or turn the page of a newspaper or magazine, or drive around town, along the highways, past billboards that compete against the scenery, crying out: "Look at me! Get my message! Go by me if you will—but then go *buy!*" You look up in the sky and a plane passes over, trailing a streamer, "The Pause That Refreshes," or a skywriter is twisting and turning while he spells out in smoke: "Not a cough in a carload!" On subway trains, streetcars, buses, railroads, steamships, taxicabs, automobiles, trucks—on everything that moves, even on jackasses, you will see signs advertising something. The mighty force of repetition—repetition—*repetition!* You may have a poor memory but you're never permitted to forget an advertised product, even for a day!

Think back. Through the science of repetition, you learned the alphabet, how to multiply. A-B-C . . . two times two are four . . . c-a-t spells *cat*. . . Tap, tap, tap! until you've got it—or it's got *you!*

Everything you've ever memorized was impressed upon your consciousness through repetition. You are constantly (tap, tap, tap) being reminded to reaffirm (more tap, tap) your faith in your religious belief. The same science, again and again. Repetition, reiteration. Tap, tap, tap!

Arthur Schopenhauer said, "There is no absurdity so palpable but that it may be firmly planted in the human head if you only begin to inculcate it before the age of five, by constantly repeating it with an air of great solemnity."

The connection between the conscious and the subconscious or subjective mind is close. Every student of the subject knows what may be accomplished by definitely contacting the subconscious. When you get a specific detailed picture in your conscious mind by using this process of reiteration or repetition, and make the subconscious mind click, you have at your command the power that astounds.

Skilled prosecutors, clever defenders appeal to the emotions of the jurors, never to the conscious reason. And how do they do it? Simply by the process of repeating and emphasizing, time after time, the points they wish to stress. They do it with usage of words and variations of argument and tones of voice, dripping with emotion. Behind all, there is that tap, tap, tap—tapping the subconscious—making the jurors believe. They've heard it again and again . . . it must be so!

It is important to stay with your idea, once you get it and feel that it is right. Repeat it over and over. Get your husband or wife or close friend to visualize with you, if he or she is in harmony and sympathy with your desired objectives. That's how power is generated.

Use the tap, tap system!

When you have the picture firmly in mind, begin using the tap, tap system, as I have outlined. It is going to be the repetition, the reiteration of that picture upon the subconscious mind that will cause the creative power within to produce results for you.

The world's most successful men and women live daily with their ideas. They hold their objectives constantly in mind. It isn't just a case with them of picturing something once, and then forgetting about it. Theirs is no wishy-washy or dilly-dally approach. They mean business. They expect to reach their goals, they are willing to work day and night, if necessary, to get there, and they have faith that this power within is working right along with them, giving them guidance in the form of urges to move in the right direction, magnetizing conditions around them, attracting resources and opportunities in accordance with their needs!

You can measure the intensity of your own desires in comparison. How much of a price in effort and sacrifice are you willing to pay to attain the things you want in life? Are you willing to try to accomplish something over and over again, until by repetition, out of seeming failure, you gain the experience and the ability to achieve? If you are, you must eventually succeed. Nothing can stop you. All obstacles must yield to your will, your drive, your faith, your God-given creative power, if you persist. But you must realize at the start that you can't get something for nothing. The universe doesn't operate this way. You must give out in effort and in faith, if you wish to receive.

Tap, tap, tap—visualizing what you want over and over—little drops of water, the endless pounding of the sea on the beach, the tramp, tramp of feet on stone stairs, cause and effect . . . cause and effect . . . action always brings about reaction. . . . You can't notice it at first, but the forces of nature and of mind, centered on any obstacle, can move that obstacle in time, or wear it away, or change it.

Harness your power to faith

Faith can move mountains, mountains of fear and doubt and worry, faith repeated again and again—faith in yourself, faith in the God Power within. It's a simple, silent, unspectacular operation, if you view it at any second, but over a long time span what you accomplish will astound you.

Now, you are the sum total of what you believe, good and bad; what you have accepted in mind, what is motivating your thoughts and acts as a result of your beliefs. As your beliefs change, your life will change with them, for your life is really based upon faith.

You have faith, every day, that you are going to keep on breathing, that your heart will continue beating, that you are alive and well. If this faith is upset, your health is upset. You have faith in everything around you . . . your work, your friends, your ability, your car, your future. You've accepted all this as a part of your life. You visualize a continuance of it all as it has been in the past. Each day you add the repetition, in general, of another similar experience. You get more and more in the groove of whatever you are doing and this may be bad, if you are doing little that is worth while. It can be good if you are applying yourself as you should.

Take inventory and make sure that what you are repeating, day after day, is helping you grow in experience, in ability, in achievement, in personal satisfaction and happiness. If it is not, you will not wish to go on repeating these activities and interests. You may want to break away from them and start a new cycle of development for yourself.

Remember: what man has done once he will do again, because he is a creature of habit. Bad thoughts are easily repeated because like always attracts like. Whatever thoughts you take into consciousness will not feel at home unless they can find similar thoughts to keep them company. What kind of thoughts are you entertaining? Are they the kind that can lead you to things you don't want to do, to experiences you don't want to have? If they are, throw them out *now,* before they become deeply entrenched through repetition.

An excessive drinker finds it difficult to stop drinking because the habit of drink has been so long impressed upon body and mind. He "sees" himself taking another drink so vividly that it becomes a gigantic task to picture himself not drinking.

The pictures you hold of yourself in mind today have only to do with your past. If you don't take charge and create new pictures of yourself, you will only repeat tomorrow what you have done today and yesterday.

Most human beings, unhappily, are on a treadmill of their own making, ending up each day where they were yesterday, although seeming to make progress because they have been moving about. But the merry-go-round always ends up at the same place unless you take stock of where you are going, get off the rotating platform by visualizing a new direction and purpose in life, and then take the high road toward greater and greater happiness and success, which can never be reached on a carrousel.

Tap, tap, tap! Is the tap, tapping that is going on in your consciousness producing more of the same for you . . . or is it the kind of tap, tapping—repetition of pictures—that is impressing right thoughts and right actions upon your subconscious?

You are the only one who knows. You are the only one who can do anything about it! Learn to use the great power of repetition in the right way, and all things shall be added unto you!

8

LISTEN TO THE VOICE WITHIN

Mahatma Gandhi upon arriving in England to seek a solution of India's problems, said: "I'm doing this because a voice within me speaks."

Gandhi referred to "something" from within. Call it a power, call it something supernatural, call it anything you wish. Some refer to it as the subjective mind. Others call it the subconscious mind. Some, universal thought. Still others refer to the impulses coming from within as hunches. Divine messages. Spiritualists refer to it as a voice from beyond. No matter what it is, it gets results, and you should learn how to acquire it.

I don't mean a voice that you hear externally. I'm sure Gandhi didn't mean this, either. But "something" within spoke to him, unmistakably, recognizably, positively; and when it spoke, Gandhi followed the directions he received, followed them to England, and would have followed them anywhere. He knew that this "voice within" could be depended upon for guidance, that when he properly prepared his mind to "hear" this voice, he could await, with expectation and confidence, a definite message.

Gandhi didn't try to force this "voice" to speak to him at any certain time, or to influence what it might say by wishful thinking. Gandhi was a spiritual leader of great humility and self-abnegation. He always placed purpose and principle above his personal needs or desires. Therein lay his great power over governments and people. They had nothing they could offer him except— justice. They knew they couldn't bargain; that when they came into the presence of this saintly man, they had to face . . . the truth. No matter how much pressure they tried to put upon Gandhi, he never moved until the "voice within" spoke.

You will do well to cultivate this "voice." All great men and women listen to it. They may not describe this inner direction in the same words, and the "voice," to them, may be an indefinable feeling or conviction which always comes when important decisions have to be made, *if* they make themselves quiet without and within, and just *listen.*

It's hard to listen! As a child, you may have felt you had to shout and kick up a rumpus before anyone paid any attention to you. As an adult, you may have gained a measure of success in the world by overshadowing and dominating. If so, developing the art of listening with your inner ear and your inner mind for counsel that comes from your deeper self, the God part of you, a higher intelligence, or whatever you choose to call it, will not be easy.

The late Thomas A. Edison was an adept at listening to this "inner voice." When he was working on an invention, trying to get the basic idea that would make the invention function, he would accumulate all the known facts with his conscious mind and then lie down on a bench or couch in his laboratory and wait for the idea to "flash to him out of thin air."

Edison's assistants would keep plugging away while the "old man" was taking a "cat nap." But Edison would eventually get up with the answer. He sometimes had to take quite a number of "cat naps" before the answer came; but it always came that way, when Edison was prepared through proper research and had stimulated the creative power sufficiently, to supply the answer to him.

How Edison did it!

A newspaper story, dated October 21, 1931, tells how Edison, working with his two associates of more than fifty years' standing, Fred Ott and Charles Dally, finally solved the secret of making synthetic rubber.

The news article says: "On Monday, he [Mr. Edison] started to sink into a stupor. [He was giving the "voice within" an opportunity to speak to him.] But Dally and Ott were still pounding doggedly at their experiments. And, on Tuesday night, the solution flashed out of the mysterious nothingness." (This is a fine way to refer to Edison's inner mind or the inner minds of his associates!)

What happened, very plainly, was that the creative power within the minds of these three scientists finally produced the answer they had been seeking. This answer came like a "bolt from the blue." It was not the result of any conscious thinking or cogitating. *Wham*—and there

102

it was! The inner voice had spoken . . . crystallizing and distilling all their past work, now stored in consciousness, and presenting to these men, in a flash, the answer to their problem: how to make synthetic rubber!

The little voice always speaks when you make up your mind what you want, and when you go after it. It is only when you are undecided, disturbed, upset, worried, doubtful or fearsome that you can't hear the "voice within." You drown it out with your own static or interference.

If your own little inner voice suggests that you ask for something, do not be backward about asking. You have nothing to fear. The other person will never help unless he knows your wishes, so you must ask. Or if you feel you should speak to someone about something, don't hesitate. Go and do it!

A man wrote me from England that he had been reading *The Magic of Believing* and that it had already altered his life. He said: "I was being used by someone in an indirect way to do something that I did not believe in. I was most unhappy about this but I did not want to anger the person who was doing this. (Fear, you see, held me back.) All of a sudden, while I was weeding my garden and thinking about this situation, something seemed to come over me—an *inner voice* spoke and gave me orders and I was no longer afraid. I dropped my hoe and went and told this person just what I thought and I have been able to stop this persecution, as a result. I tell you, I've felt like a different person ever since!"

Learn to recognize your inner voice

When the "inner voice" really speaks, it is a sign you are ready to *act*. Drop your hoe, as this man from England did, or whatever you are doing, and do what you feel impelled to do. But be sure you have learned to recognize the "inner voice" and that it is not just your wishful thinking or imagination or fears talking to you.

Joan of Arc was just a French peasant girl but she heard the "voice" speak. Following its direction, she inspired the French to drive the English out of Orleans and enabled Charles to be proclaimed king at Rheims.

Jesus heard "the voice of God speak to Him" and acted upon this inner guidance to lead all mankind to higher spiritual attainments.

Abraham Lincoln, in the small hours of the night, during the critical hours of the Civil War, listened to the "voice within" and because of the messages he received arrived at many grave decisions, which saved our Union.

Mark Twain's characters used to talk to him. He heard their dialogue spoken in his mind and simply wrote it down. Mark Twain placed great reliance on his intuitive powers, he believed in hunches, and always listened to "the voice."

To get ideas from your own subjective or subconscious mind, you must be able to make your conscious mind receptive. Of course, we all know it is the conscious mind which reasons, which weighs, which calculates. The subconscious mind does not do any of these things. It simply passes on ideas to the conscious mind.

You have probably heard people say, "Play your

hunches." What are these hunches? Where do they come from? They come from the workings of the subconscious mind. Psychologists tell us that to put the human mind in a receptive condition, you must relax. If you have ever lain on the massage table and been told by the masseur to relax, then you know what I mean.

Let the body go limp. If you have trouble at first, try it with your arm, both arms, both legs, until the whole body is gone over and relaxed. The mind will automatically let go then, too. When that is accomplished, concentrate on what you want; then hunches come. Grab them, execute them as the little voice tells you. Do not reason or argue, but do as you are told and do it immediately.

You will understand what psychologists, mystics and students mean when they tell you to stop, relax—*think of nothing*—when you wish to draw on the subconscious and have the little inner voice speak. As you further progress, you will also begin to realize what the seers of the East had in mind when they said:

"Become at ease, meditate, go into the great silence, continue to meditate, and your problems will fade into nothingness."

The road ahead will become illuminated and your burdens will fall away, one by one. Is there anything clearer than *Pilgrim's Progress?* My message is no different from that which Bunyan conveyed there. Only, as I have said before, I am putting it to you in different words.

The "voice within" can guide you, asleep or awake, if you train yourself to rely upon it. A young housewife in Fort Worth, Texas, was awakened one night with a feeling of great urgency. The "voice within" told her to get up and look about the apartment. Her husband and baby were sleeping, everything appeared to be all right, but she couldn't get over this uneasy, apprehensive sensation. To quiet her nerves, she got out of bed and found herself directed to the bathroom. Nothing seemed to be wrong but she felt impelled to flush the toilet. The instant she did so, hot water rushed out, followed by clouds of steam. The pipes began to pound. She aroused her husband and he phoned for help just in time. Something had gone wrong with the thermostat control in the basement, and had this not been discovered, the boiler would have blown up in the next few minutes and wrecked the entire apartment house!

Follow the urgings of your voice

Give heed to your hunches when they come, whenever they come. Don't turn a deaf ear to the "voice within." Your inner mind is aware of conditions and things that your conscious mind knows nothing about.

You've heard people say, "Something told me that I should beware of that person or I should have done this or shouldn't have done that . . . but I didn't pay any attention until it was too late. I wish I'd followed those hunches and feelings now."

It's there—"that something"—trying to serve you in many ways, if you will let it. A widow who wanted to find the right man and marry again had the urge to leave New York City and go to California and buy a home. She went to visit friends in Long Beach who took her around to property that was for sale. She fell in love with a house owned by a widower who, in turn, fell in love with her. Instead of buying his home she married the widower, and got the home, anyway. They are one of the happiest married couples today that I know. In this case, the "voice within" led her three thousand miles to bring her an answer to her desire.

But don't *you* travel three thousand miles, expecting to find romance, unless you get the same clear direction which came to this woman. *Your* romance may be right around the corner from you, waiting on a bus, in a store, in a dentist's office, a park, a library, at a social occasion. But if you picture meeting the right man or woman for you, strongly enough and persistently enough, you will get the urge to be at the right place at the right time so that the two of you can be brought together. Remember! Like always attracts like! And someone is looking for you just as eagerly as you are looking for him or for her. Since your subconscious minds are not limited by time or space, you'll make contact, sooner or later, and the "inner voice" will tell each of you, "He or she is the one for me."

You do not actually "hear" the voice within

Occasionally I meet men or women who tell me, in all seriousness, that they "hear voices." This is quite different from the "voice of guidance" and is often the sign of a hallucinatory condition which they have developed through some emotional upset or nervous affliction. Such a state is not to be desired and should be guarded against.

These voices are so "real" to the people who hear them that they are convinced they are either obsessed by some disincarnate entity or some real-life individual who has designs on them. When this condition exists, they are usually terrorized by it.

I was in the office of Johnny Neblett, a radio commentator, one time in Chicago, when an attractive young woman came in, unannounced, and said to him: "Well, here I am. You've been calling to me and I have come. What do you want with me?"

Mr. Neblett stared at the young woman in amazement, then decided that this was a "gag" of some kind, and laughed.

"This is no laughing matter," said the woman, highly incensed. "I can't sleep nights . . . you're always talking to me. I hear your voice all the time. You've got to stop it. You're driving me crazy!"

This sobered Johnny in a hurry and he turned nervously to me for help.

"This man is a psychologist," he said, introducing me to the woman. "I haven't been calling you or talking to you. I never saw you before. I'm sure it's all in your mind. He can explain it to you."

Just as easy as that! I was handed *some* assignment. This young woman, quite obviously, was emotionally unbalanced and had developed a fixation on the commentator from listening to him on the radio. Something in his voice appealed to her, aroused her emotionally, and she had mesmerized herself into thinking she heard his voice "inside her head," as she put it.

"If I'm thinking of him all the time I might as well

be with him," she insisted. "He's lying. He really wants me. He has attracted me telepathically. He doesn't need to have seen me before. His mind is so strong that he can reach me and make me do what he wants."

It took several hours to convince this woman that the voice she thought she heard was a creation of her own emotionally disturbed consciousness. During this time she had accused the commentator of having designs upon her and demanded that he "release" her.

When she was finally straightened out and left, considerably embarrassed, apologizing for the trouble she had caused, and thanking me for freeing her from her delusion, my commentator friend almost had a nervous collapse himself.

"One more case like that," he said, "and I give up radio!"

I cite this experience to make it very, very clear that the "voice within" has no connection whatsoever with this kind of voice. It is not a voice, actually, in the external sense of the word. It is an intelligence, a sudden idea or knowledge or intuitive flash which communicates with you from the subconscious and gives you an urge, a definite feeling of what to do or say or in what direction to move with respect to some problem or situation.

You can, with a little practice and training, always distinguish a hunch or the "voice within" from the way you feel when your imagination or your wishful thinking tries to cook up something for you. This difference in feeling cannot be put in words, but you'll recognize it. You won't let yourself be carried away with the wrong impressions. You'll know, deep down within yourself, when the real you is talking to you, from the center of your being . . . the creative center.

Then, like Gandhi, you will act, with confidence, in meeting any life experience as it should be met, saying to yourself: "I am doing this because a voice within me speaks."

9

DECIDE WHAT YOU WANT

There is no more miserable human being than one in whom nothing is habitual but indecision.

WILLIAM JAMES

There can be no gainsaying that once you have made up your mind to do a thing, it will be done. But the trouble with most of us is that we sidestep, vacillate, backtrack, detour and seldom make up our minds to do what we want or determine clearly the road on which we wish to travel.

All daydreams and wishes could become realities if we kept them constantly before us, put fear behind, shoved away all reservations, ifs, ands and buts. Again, many of us think we know what we want when, as a matter of fact, we don't. This sounds paradoxical, but if we all knew what we wanted, we would get it, provided we had the will power, the stamina, the dynamic force, the fight to go after it.

The world is divided into two classes of people: the "I Will-ers" and the "Should-I-or-Shouldn't-I-ers"; and this latter class includes the great majority of men and women.

How many times have you said to yourself: "Should I or shouldn't I?" More human lives have been wrecked on the shoals of indecision than from any other cause.

"That something"—the creative power within—cannot magnetically attract things to you unless it is magnetized by your decision. A magnet cannot attract in two directions at once. Its magnetic force must be centered upon some definite object. You can demonstrate this by passing a magnet over a pile of iron filings. When you point the magnetized end of the magnet at any specific place in the pile, the iron filings are drawn instantly to it. Move the magnet away from this section and its power diminishes in proportion to the distance and direction.

When you are pulling against yourself, mentally and emotionally, you are confusing, stalemating and even destroying your magnetic powers of attraction, for the time being.

An unsettled condition of mind and body can only attract unsettled conditions. It has no power to attract anything else.

The great lament of thousands upon thousands of human beings is: "I can't make up my mind!" This is one of the saddest dirges ever to rise from human hearts because it sounds the death knell of hope, ambition, self-confidence, initiative, accomplishment.

As long as you can't make up your mind you are comparatively helpless, unable to move in any direction with assurance or with any feeling of safety and security.

"My mind is like an unmade bed," one woman said to me, "it's all in a jumble. I'm afraid to make it up—I'm afraid to touch it—for fear I'll make it even worse. I guess I'll just leave it as it is!"

Do you wish to remain where you now are? If you do, just don't make up your mind! Unless you change your thinking, you will stay in whatever position you find yourself. Either that, or you will sink to a lower position because nothing stands still in life. It moves either up or down. Metal rusts if nothing is done to keep it polished and free of disintegrating forces.

You can't drop behind in the parade of life. You must keep going, for your own sake, at any age. Nature abhors anything that surrenders its usefulness. The buzzards are always waiting to do a clean-up job on forms of life that give up the struggle. Sounds pretty grim? It's not meant to be. Something has been provided to take care of everything, in all the various stages of life activity and what is called death. In your body, millions of old cells are dying and new cells are being born, all the time. You are unconscious of it.

The same is true of ideas. As you grow in experience, you are killing off old ideas in your mind and giving birth to new ones. If you don't do this, the old, out-moded ideas clog up your mind, slow up your thinking, rust your brain, retard your progress and eventually bog you down.

If you are finding that you can't make decisions the way you used to do, it's probably because you are wrestling with old ideas, old thought patterns, old habits and desires which you can't let go of, even when your "voice within" tells you to throw them overboard, get out of the rut and get to doing what you inwardly know you *should* be doing.

"Have you come to the Red Sea place in your life,
Where, in spite of all you can do,
There is no way out, there is no way back,
There is no other way but through?"

Annie Johnson Flint

If this is your state of mind and situation in life at the moment, it is good! If your back is against the wall, if you've been pushed by indecision and circumstances of your own conscious or unconscious creation, as far as you can go, then there is "no other way but through."

So face reality. Reorient yourself, reorganize your scattered forces, *make up your mind*, and move straight ahead!

Decide—then act!

Many men and women have reached the seeming limit of their endurance only to find new strength awaiting them in their hours of desperate need, once they reached a positive decision—once they said to themselves, and meant it, "I'll face it. I'll see this thing through!"

There is no eleventh hour too late wherein "that something," the creative power within, cannot be magnetized by right thought and right decision and give you the strength and wisdom to pull out.

"God spoke to me in my great moment of need," thousands of grateful men and women have testified. They mean that they finally were driven to call upon their God-given inner resources after trying everything else and failing . . . and the inner power which they might have used all along answered their summons!

Don't make the mistake of thinking that you can ever succeed by using your conscious mind alone. The egotist likes to pretend he's done it all himself, through sheer will power and physical force. He pats himself on the back and says, "Look at me. I'm a self-made man!" But let this egotist suffer a setback in business or his private life and watch his ego deflate. He goes around with his hat pulled down around his ears, his chin stuck down in his coat collar, his eyes staring at the ground, mumbling to himself, "I can't understand how this could have happened to me!"

Oh, yes, you can get somewhere on your own physical drive, by conscious connivance, manipulation, a cleverness of wit, deceit and a "it's-who-you-know" philosophy. But what you gain by force, you eventually lose by force. You have no staying power. Someone else, using the same dog-eat-dog tactics, kicks you off the road or steamrollers you. Then, because you have misused your real powers within—if you have used them at all—you are lost! For the first time in your life, perhaps, you are scared. You have no more faith in the methods you employed to get where you were . . . and you have little or no faith in your fellow man or in God. The world is a pretty barren place and you are the most barren creature in it. Worst of all, your confidence in self and in everything else has been so shattered that you can't decide what to do about it.

Stop bemoaning your fate—get wise to yourself!

You have only two choices. You can either go higher or lower. You may take to drink or help yourself to a first-class nervous breakdown or wander around through the rest of your life, moaning about "what might have been" if you had only lived your life differently—but telling yourself, "it's too late now."

But if you belong to that smaller percentage of men and women who have "gotten wise to themselves," you discover that it is never too late to get on the right track. You discover that you have been passing up the most wonderful force in your life, the creative power within, which has been ready and willing, at all times, to serve you.

A deep feeling of humility steals over you, and you lose your falsely assumed attitudes of egotism and self-importance forever. Once you are down to bedrock, you find that you have a foundation on which to build, that you can pick up your life again and make something of it, something finer than ever before, perhaps not so flashy or so gaudy, but so much more worthwhile, self-satisfying, healthful and enjoyable. Now, at last, you can decide what is best for you, without worrying what the other fellow is going to do to you unless, perhaps, you do it to him first. There has come to you the inner assurance that whatever you really need can and will be supplied to you by your creative power, if you keep in attunement with it, and direct it by right mental picturing. Not only this but you realize that you have been missing out on many things in life of far greater value than many of the things you thought you had to have a short time ago.

Perhaps, in a radical sense, you do not fit into this category just depicted. But in a lesser sense, we all fit. It is human to make mistakes, human to permit certain emotional desires to get the better of us, to carry us far afield from our real purposes and potentialities in life.

"I knew better but I did it anyway," many sadder and wiser people say, after they have gotten a new hold on themselves and snapped out of their departure from sane, happy, healthful living.

If you have reached the snap-back stage: *now* is the time. There is no other time for you but *now*. If you don't do it now, you'll never do it. You have reached your moment of decision!

"There is no way out, there is no way back, there is no other way but through!"

Take the plunge! Pull yourself out! Face whatever you have to face—and get it over with. The longer you delay, the harder it will be.

Decision always magnetizes!

Decision starts an immediate magnetic action in your mind which rearranges the iron filings of your life, reassembles the broken pieces, fits them together into a new fabric, strengthens the weak spots, and gives you new vitality and resolution to do what the "inner voice" dictates. Take direction from your real self within, follow its urgings no matter how difficult it may seem at the moment, ask forgiveness of those you have wronged, clear up all past resentments and hatreds, free your consciousness of past fears and inhibitions, so your mind can become a channel for good thoughts and can begin to help you attract good things to you!

Get away forever from David Harum's indecisive: "Yes, an' no, an' mebbe, an' mebbe not!"

This will never get you anywhere. Who wants to live a miserable "yes an' no" and "mebbe an' mebbe not" existence?

"I'd rather make a wrong decision and do something about it than make no decision at all," a successful business man said to me. "If I'm on my toes, I can usually tell whether a decision is wrong or not, before it hurts me too much—and out of this wrong decision, I then have the wisdom to make a right one. But if I make no decision at all, I get nowhere."

It takes courage and faith to make many decisions, but the happy, well-integrated man or woman is he or she who dares to act, without hesitation, on the basis of the best judgment and intuition at the moment.

Joseph Addison is credited with the statement: "The woman that deliberates is lost."

What indecision does!

I am thinking now of a woman who was in love with two men at the same time. Both wanted to marry her and she kept them dangling, unable to make a decision between them, for over a year. Finally she made her choice, but confided to her mother on her wedding day that she feared she had made a mistake. She carried this uncertainty into her marriage, always wondering whether or not she would have been happier with the other man. This "would I or wouldn't I" mental state upset her emotionally and reflected upon her sexual relations with her husband. She became frigid, worrying about the decision she had made, afraid to confess her real feelings to her mate. But one night, in utter exasperation, he exploded: "I wish to hell you had married Bill!" And she impulsively cried out, "I wish the hell I had, too!"

This release of tension, bringing the subject out into the open, helped her to face herself. She realized then that she had been giving herself a fictitious build-up, that her quality of indecision had caused her to divide her emotional feelings between the two men, and if any little thing went wrong in the association between the man she had chosen and herself, she pictured, to salve her own hurt feelings, a perfect relationship existing between herself and the man she had not married.

"I'm sure now that I really love you," she told her husband, "that I didn't make any mistake when something inside told me that you were the one. I'm sorry I've been so silly and juvenile about things—but it's pretty hard to break the habits of a lifetime!"

Make your positive decision now!

If indecision has you in its grip . . . *break* this lifetime habit. If you don't, you'll be miserable the rest of your life and your percentage of wrong decisions will attract many more wrong conditions to you.

The "voice within" cannot get through to you when you are in an emotional and mental state of indecision.

A preacher relative of mine became disturbed in thought when a young man. His studies led him to doubt certain parts of the Bible. He began to censure himself for teaching what he could no longer believe. This developed a conflict within him, a plaguing wonderment: "Am I doing right or wrong by continuing in the ministry?" Finally he developed asthma and would get attacks just before going into the pulpit on Sunday. It was Nature's way of keeping him from saying what he felt he shouldn't say. His body was reflecting a condition of his mind. He finally retired from the ministry on the plea of ill health, not confessing his religious misgivings even to his wife. For thirty years, this highly intelligent man lived a life of torture. The asthmatic attacks would be most severe at times when he was wrestling with himself over sins of omission and commission. "Did I do right or didn't I?"

I had a talk with this relative near the end of his life. He said that he just had to get something off his mind. When he had told me what had been troubling him all these years, he wanted to know if I thought he would be damned for this. I assured him that I thought the God Power in this universe was too big and understanding to condemn or to damn any human being . . . that we all made mistakes . . . that this was the only way any of us could grow, through mistakes. Then he said to me: "Oh, if I only had my life to live over. I would have left the church and I would have turned to writing and expressed my convictions, honestly, openly, because I realize now, too late, that many men and women had been thinking as I was thinking. But I let fear and indecision and self-condemnation keep me from my *real* life work!"

Many people, when confronted with two possible courses of action and not sure which is right, try to do both—usually to their sorrow. No one has been able to go very far in two directions at the same time. You must make a choice, and you can generally make the right choice, if you will let the "voice within" guide you. But it is always tempting to listen to the voice of our emotions, our personal or prejudiced desires—which too often lead us astray.

Shakespeare had his Hamlet say what many of us, in our troubled minds, have said:

"To be, or not to be: that is the question:
Whether 'tis nobler in the mind to suffer
The slings and arrows of outrageous fortune,
Or to take arms against a sea of troubles,
And by opposing end them? . . ."

(And then to paraphrase):

. . . But then the dread of what may happen . . .
Makes us rather bear those ills we have
Than fly to others that we know not of. . . .

How easy it is, when we are beset with ills of one kind and another, to picture *greater* ills . . . and to decide to put up with the ills we have, rather than attempt to rise above them—and thus, we fear, encounter "other ills we know not of"!

Decision is born of courage and courage springs from faith in self and in the God Power within. Why go on picturing a continuation of the problems and conditions which may be surrounding you now?

Decide to do away with them by resolutely changing the pictures, thus giving "that something" within the power to change your future—for the better!

10

WRITE IT DOWN

What your eyes see and your ears hear, if seen and heard often enough, you remember . . . and make a part of your life.

Scientists and advertisers both recognize this fact in their use of "visual aids" and recordings to impress the minds of different groups of people.

Some people are influenced more by what they see, others by what they hear. It depends upon which sense they have developed the habit, in childhood, of utilizing most.

You may be on a car trip with someone and keep on noticing things, in passing, which the other person does not see. He or she is not trained in observation, as you are, but might say to you, "Did you hear that?" And you may reply, "No—what?" There are varying degrees of sensitivity in sight and hearing.

"I was criticized so much when I was a child that I didn't want to hear what was said about me, so I don't hear now as well as I should," a man said to me.

"When I was a little girl," a woman related, "I saw something I shouldn't have seen. This shocked me so that ever since I have been afraid to use my eyes any more than I need to see what I have to see. I find that I am not paying attention to many things taking place around me because I inwardly feel it's none of my business and that I shouldn't be noticing them."

Inhibitions are one of the great self-inflicted plagues of the human race but we all have our share, in one form or another. It is almost impossible not to have taken on some, during the growing-up process.

As adults, however, we should have the intelligence to recognize and to eliminate as many of these emotional tie-ups as possible, so we can be freed of their destructive influence over us.

Picturing the things you want to have and do in life is therefore a good method of crystallizing and pinpointing your desires so that your mind can better focus its attention upon them. And the more you can keep the picture or pictures before you, the more impressed the power within will be to help you materialize them.

For this reason, I recommend, as an aid in the visualization of the things you want, in order to keep them uppermost in your thoughts, that you write a word picture of them on small cards, so you can have them where you can look at them as frequently as possible.

As a suggestion, stick one card above the mirror to be looked at in the morning when you shave, or fix your hair. Permit the details of your wishes, outlined on the card, to increase as you continue to develop the mental pictures.

Have another card convenient to look at while you

eat your lunch—your dinner. Use the cards again just before you go to sleep. Keep it up. Tap, tap, tap! However, there is no point to writing down your wishes until you have determined that every single detail of what you want is to be photographed permanently in your thoughts—to stay there until it becomes a reality.

If what you are picturing for yourself is of a personal nature, and there are people about who would not be in sympathy with your desires, or who would regard this practice as foolish, then keep your cards to yourself, and study them only when you have a spare moment and an opportunity for privacy.

Remember that *repetition* of the same thought, the same suggestion, makes the *picture* possible.

He who knows how to plant, shall not have his plant uprooted; He who knows how to hold a thing, shall not have it taken away.

Lao Tzu, the Chinese Mystic, 600 B.C.

Plant your picture in mind!

Write it down!

If you have the desire, the foundation is laid. Plant the picture in mind! A perfectly detailed picture of the exact thing, or things, you wish. It won't hurt to picture more than one objective at a time, as long as they are not in conflict, and as long as you can picture them separately. The creative power within can work on as many projects as you desire and to which you can give your attention and your efforts!

Write it down!

If it is increased sales you want, fix the exact amounts;

if it's something you want the other fellow to do for you, the love of a woman or that of a man, a new suit of clothes or a new automobile, write it down. Anything and every-thing—write it down.

Express in your own words what you want. It will help your mind to get organized on it. No matter what you are after under this system, you can have it—*provided the object of desire is morally right, and the picture definite and positive!*

Tap–tap–tap–tap! Write it down, again and again, if you find this helps you fix your goal in mind.

It matters not whether you be a salesman, an execu-tive, a mechanic, a writer, a housewife or what—whether you are after money, love, improvement in social posi-tion, in the legal profession or medical profession—it makes absolutely no difference. You have that same power in you, ready to bring you what you want. You can acquire every single thing you desire . . . a pair of shoes or a mansion. You name it, write it down, and go to work on it!

Opportunities are constantly flowing past you in the stream of life unless you reach out and grab them! If you don't know what you're looking for, how can you get it?

Every way you can express what you desire, in writ-ing, in voice, in pictures, helps vitalize the creative power within and keeps your thoughts magnetized on the target.

Some men and women keep a large envelope labeled, "My Heart's Desires," in which they keep written state-ments of what they want, of changes they wish to make in their lives, economically, personally, physically, mentally, spiritually. They put aside certain times during the day or evening when they get off by themselves and reread and reflect upon the different written expressions of heartfelt desires. They also check each one, and take inventory to see if they have made progress toward their respective goals. When they reach a certain objective they mark the case "closed" and write on the card an expression of their thanks to the God Power within for helping them realize their dream. Then they go on to something else, constantly unfolding and developing. It is an endless, glorious, satisfying process!

If you are just starting, you will need to remake your thinking, eliminating many wrong thoughts and emotional reactions which are already in consciousness. To do this, it will be helpful for you to write down what you now realize should be your right attitude toward others, toward money, business, any and everything of importance that you have to deal with in your everyday life.

Marjorie Mayes, a dynamically successful businesswoman in San Francisco, attributes much of her success and the wide circle of devoted friends whom she enjoys, to the written word. She has defined her attitude toward "business," toward the earning and meaning of money. She rereads this statement, "The Know in Business," every day as a formula to live by. Then she listens for "the voice within" to direct her life.

Marjorie Mayes has consented to let me share her inspired statement with you:

THE KNOW IN BUSINESS

Pray at all times knowing Right prayers are answered. . . . Anything that ever is, is forever God's. . . . All that I am is God, and I am part of

God . . . therefore nothing but Divine harmony is expressed in my life. . . . I individualize God and have direct contact with Truth. . . . My intuition is perfect, my Spiritual perception is perfect. . . . I know God is my wisdom, my intelligence, so I am always directed to Right action at all times . . . as God is the only Doer. God works through me, therefore, I am always working Rightly and there is no danger of any harm to anyone because of my negotiations. . . . There is no waste of time for God's work is my work, therefore, my work is well and unselfishly done. . . . My thoughts are clear, new, fresh and powerful results are felt in my work. . . . My ever praying thoughts are the handiwork of God, powerful as the Eagle that flies over the universe with direction, in season, yet as gentle, humble and nonaggressive as the Dove. . . . My prayers go forth in all my negotiations in the name of God and I, therefore, cannot close a single day empty-handed. . . . My prayers are powerful and I know they will accomplish that which I accept as Right Action. . . . I know every relation in life will be found to depend upon my ability to see God in action in my life and prayers. . . . I am not dependent on man or conditions, I am dependent upon Substance, Spirit, therefore, I do not look to man or conditions but to the Infinite for direction. . . . I listen to my intuitions, which is accepting God. . . . My eyes are fixed on appreciation of God's gifts and I do not place money apart from those gifts, therefore, money loves being in my purse because I spend with God's wisdom. . . . I receive money through Right Action in all my deals. . . . I do not bargain with God. . . . I do not tell God how money must come to me . . . I just negotiate, listening to my own intuitions, knowing that it is done unto us as we believe.

Marjorie Mayes

This is a magnificent statement of one person's mental and spiritual attitude toward life—toward others, toward business, toward money . . . and this statement can be yours!

Make a copy of it and read and reread it . . . take it into your consciousness . . . make it a part of *you*. Write it down—speak it—listen to yourself say it . . . believe it, live it through Right Action as applied to your own needs . . . and, as Marjorie Mayes says, "it will be done unto you as you believe!"

Think of pictures you have seen, paintings, photographs, landscapes—pictures of people doing things—activities of various kinds. How many of these pictures do you remember? How many stand out in memory—and why? I'll tell you. Because something in those you remember caught your personal interest and held it, you saw something of yourself and your doings in them, you felt a kinship for some feature in them, these pictures made such an impression on you that you never forgot them. In fact, these pictures and other pictures you have seen, and countless pictures you yourself have created in your imagination, are still making an impression on you in consciousness . . . where everything you have ever seen or heard or experienced continues to exist in picture form!

The feelings associated with these pictures are also influencing you. In fact, it is your feeling reaction to whatever has happened to you that influences you most of all. How deeply you feel about anything you desire determines how intensely the creative power within magnetizes conditions around you and attracts what you wish to you. Obviously, if you deeply fear something may happen to you, it will cause this creative power to work just as magnetically to attract what you fear to you.

Write fear out of your life by writing down affirmations of courage and faith and self-assurance. You know and believe good things are going to happen. You are ruling all fear and worry thoughts out of consciousness. You realize, if you permit them to remain, that they can only attract unhappy conditions.

Your conscious mind is a sieve and a filter at the same time. It takes everything that happens to you in this outer world into it and passes it on to the subconscious in the form of mental pictures. That's its normal, automatic process, unless you stop certain pictures and alter them, or don't permit what you recognize as a wrong picture to go through!

Now this thought is going to come as a shocker! The uncontrolled conscious mind of any individual is little more than an open sewer which takes in all manner of refuse and debris in the form of wrong thoughts and feelings, along with the good. Unless you stand guard over what you take in, there is no sifting, no filtering of the good from the bad. It all goes into your inner consciousness. And what goes in must eventually come out in the same form, or remain within to attract more of the same . . . because like always attracts like!

You've heard of the "stream-of-consciousness"

That's a pretty accurate description. Thoughts are streaming into and out of your mind all the time.

Control the nature of your pictures!

Warning: Don't let your stream of consciousness become any more polluted than it is! Put up your *filter screen*. Stop all fear and worry thoughts, all wrong emotional reactions before they get into your inner consciousness where they can do you untold damage. Begin to screen out the wrong thoughts and feelings that are already floating around in the stream of your subconscious. Bail them out. Get rid of them. Clear up this stream so it can reflect the good, clean thoughts you are now sending in upon the waters of your life experience.

Write down what you want to be. Write out of your life what you don't want to be!

Constant practice of writing down your wishes and using a mirror will work wonders. Shortly you can form the pictures at will, without the use of either cards or mirrors, and you will find yourself tapping the subconscious mind almost automatically. But you still may wish to continue the writing-down technique . . . the reading and rereading of your cards.

Practice—practice—always keep tapping!

Don't be afraid of overdoing, or becoming extravagant with your wishes and desires because, as I have said before, you can have every single thing you wish, but you must become adept at doing exactly as I tell you.

When you visualize and keep the pictures constant, action follows because action, after all, is nothing more than *energized* thought.

Never lose your vision (your mental pictures) for, as King Solomon said nearly three thousand years ago: "Where there is no vision, the people perish."

Bear in mind that this whole theme is as old as man. I am merely giving you the message in words of today and outlining a simple system of mechanics which may be used by anyone.

As we all know, "The proof of the pudding is in the eating." And if you have any doubts as to whether or not I am giving you an exact science, *try* it! The automobile will begin to take shape, you will get the new shoes and the bricks of the mansion will fall into place as though a magical hand had touched them.

The weight of evidence is on the side of the thousands and thousands of happy, successful, healthy men and women who have already demonstrated and are demonstrating the working of "that something"—the God-given creative power—in their daily lives!

Keep a written record of the things you want, and check against it. You'll soon be checking the things off as you attain them!

Stop your day-dreaming, eliminate your doubts, get busy, try writing down your desires. It works!

11

I KNOW IT—I BELIEVE IT— AND IT IS SO!

There's a saying I thoroughly believe in: *"If you believe it, it's so!"*

This is simply a cryptic statement or digest of what I have been telling you over and over. All the great teachers, Buddha, Confucius, Mohammed, Jesus and many philosophers taught this great fundamental idea. It is found in all religions, cults, creeds and sects. Everywhere runs the same general theme, the gist of which in my words is: *"If you believe it, it's so!"*

I quote from the Bible: *"As a man thinketh in his heart so is he."* You've heard this quotation many times before, but I repeat for emphasis: *"As a man thinketh in his heart so is he." If you believe it, it's so.* Note the similarity? Reduce the whole thing to one word: "Faith."

I have heard many, many people say the day of miracles is past, but never in my life have I heard a thinker, a student or a believer make such a declaration. Surely, the days of Aladdin and his lamp are gone, and perhaps they never existed . . . so with the magic wand, the magic carpet, and all of those things of fairy tale and legend. Entertaining but no basis in fact, no reality.

When I refer to miracles, I mean those things which can be accomplished through *faith* . . . faith in your belief; faith in yourself; faith in the persons with whom you are associated; faith in a power; faith in "that something" which controls the destinies of everyone. . . . If you can get that faith and dissipate the negative side, nothing in this world can stop you from acquiring what you desire. While this may sound facetious, it is true—you can have anything obtainable if you really want it.

Faith is the mainspring of attainment. You must have it to achieve—to move yourself—and others!

What is it that Aimee had? Gypsy Smith? Billy Sunday? The present-day Billy Graham, Monsignor Sheen, Norman Vincent Peale? *Belief—faith,* fundamentally, and the ability of a staunch believer to pass it on to the other fellow. It's the very keynote of all great religions. All big things are started by one person, one believer. It makes no difference where he got the idea originally. All great inventions are the outgrowth of the whole scheme of faith, faith, belief in yourself, your ideas, your ability to put them over. All supersalesmen know this. They use the power. That's why they are supersalesmen, of religions, commodities, projects. Every community drive, every forward movement, everything worthwhile succeeds because some one person has faith, is the prime mover, the sparkplug, the central fountain, and is able to sell what he has faith in to the multitudes—to pass faith on like a contagion. Think about that. Then think about it some more, and think of it again. Meditate over it, and you'll realize that every word is true!

You have faith in a religion, a commercial product, a community drive because someone, originally, gave you faith in it. You accept certain people as authorities because you believe in them. What they tell you, you believe, without question, and you take or buy what they offer you. That's faith.

Occasionally some clever person will mislead you and cause you to believe in something that isn't so; and when you discover this, you are often bitter and disillusioned. You say, "I'll never believe in anyone again," but you will, because to believe is a fundamental trait of human nature. You instinctively want to believe in others and in yourself. This would be a terrible world if we couldn't trust anyone.

"Foghorn" Murphy, the famous umpire baiter, said over the radio on Groucho Marx's "You Bet Your Life" show, that the "cheapest" thing a person could do was to be nice to other people, greet them with a smile and trust them—that this paid the biggest dividends. He's a thousand per cent right: genuine faith in the other fellow always pays off. You may misplace your faith a few times, but this is a rarity. Most people make an extra effort to live up to your faith in them. They may fail others, even take advantage of them, but they are so appreciative of your faith that they won't let you down.

I've had men and women say to me: "What are you wasting time on that drunken, no-good deadbeat for? He can't be depended on. He'll steal you blind or take advantage of you at the first opportunity."

Well, I've placed my faith in hundreds and hundreds of men and women thus far and I haven't been intentionally let down yet. Some of the folks I have trusted were just too weak to keep on an even keel, but they didn't go out to "take" me. They felt worse than I did about failing to live up to my estimate of them—and most of them have picked themselves up and have been trying, again and again. They know I still have faith in them . . . that I haven't condemned them . . . that I'm always willing to help, when and where I can. But they know, too, that it is basically up to them, that no person can be helped beyond a certain point, that they've got to do the job of getting back on their feet themselves, through faith.

The power within cannot operate for you unless you have faith in it!

Put your belief to work!

Experience is the greatest and, at the same time, the severest teacher. Through experience you *know* what you've done wrong, it beats in on you eventually. And after you know, you start to work setting yourself right, by realizing that you need some power greater than yourself to help straighten out your affairs and start you thinking right. So—you discover "that something" within and you say, "I believe!" And this sets up a magnetic current in you which commences to attract what you believe in. . . . And when you can feel and see coming to you the things that you have pictured, through faith, you say: ". . . and it is so!"

That's the process of rehabilitation in a nutshell. It may not be religious in any orthodox or creedal sense, but it's spiritual, metaphysical. It's what the spiritual leaders of all time have been talking about, reduced to everyday language.

There are countless organized campaigns going on whose purpose is to get you to believe in this and that—right along! Pause and think for a moment. What is propaganda, any kind of propaganda, the good and the bad? Often nothing more, nor less than well-developed, ingenious plans to make you believe. You've seen it work in previous war days, and if you're wide-awake to what is going on around you, you know that it's being worked more than ever in every line of human endeavor today; just as it was worked thousands of years ago and as it always will work.

The battle is on for the minds of men all over the world—in free and slave nations, behind and in front of iron curtains. Take great care about what you are enticed to believe in, be sure you are in unprejudiced, truthful possession of unaltered facts. If not, withhold judgment and don't permit your reason and intuition to be swept aside by convincing sounding emotional appeals.

If when you are reading your newspaper, listening to the radio, viewing television, you keep in mind my theme, you will realize that all the speeches of our leaders, our great executives, coming to us with clock-like regularity, are being given with a purpose—to make us believe. These men know this. Even so: study everything that is said today, draw your own conclusions, make up your own mind as fairly and as unprejudicedly as you can, before you believe.

Everyone of us, if put on the right track, can accomplish what he is after by keeping before him my own expression: "If you believe it—it's so," and by adopting the old adage: "Where there's a will, there's a way!"

In other words, get that will power, that faith, that belief, working every minute of the day—24 hours of the day—seven days a week—365 days a year. And I promise you, if you do you will shoot ahead of people in the progress you make as rapidly as high-frequency electrical discharges oscillate through the ether!

Belief takes you where you want to go with the speed of jet propulsion. Doubt and disbelief take you just as fast in the opposite direction. Belief always magnetizes; disbelief demagnetizes.

You know something of the efficacy of prayer. What is prayer but the expression of a heartfelt, earnest, sincere want or desire? The Great Master said:

What things soever ye desire, when ye pray believe that ye receive them, and ye shall have them.

And it's true! All of us know the effect of our own desires on ourselves and how events are influenced by great desires. Every economic change down through the centuries has been due to the desire of man to benefit himself. However, we must believe, have faith. Otherwise, our innermost desires (prayers) become simply bursting bubbles.

The Great Master also said:

If thou canst believe, all things are possible to him that believeth.

You've heard all this before, but what you have done and what are you doing about it?

Belief—faith—is something that has to take hold of you; after you take hold of it. It has to get down inside you and work from within out. When you believe sufficiently in something, you bring it into existence in your mind. The creative power within creates it for you. Then it starts to work to duplicate it in your outer life. If you don't let your fears and worries and doubts change this picture, the original pattern you gave your subconscious of what you want, there'll come a day when you'll see it materialized, just as it once was in consciousness.

Believe—have faith—and, as I have said, and say again, to impress it indelibly upon your mind: "Anything you want can be yours!"

The tremendous power of faith!

You think faith isn't practical—that it can't do the things I claim for you? Here's a real-life demonstration of the workings of faith when the odds were millions to one against any power in the universe saving this man!

Listen! In September, 1949, a nineteen-year-old Navy seaman, William Toles of Rochester, Michigan, was washed overboard from his carrier, without a life jacket. It was four o'clock in the morning and he was far out to sea, off the coast of Africa! No one saw him go overboard, and he knew when he hit the water that his chances of rescue were almost nil.

Instead, however, of surrendering to wild panic, young Toles kicked out of his dungarees, tied knots in the pants legs, and used the seat of the pants as a wind-trap to inflate the legs, thus fashioning himself an impro-vised life jacket.

In his own story, Bill Toles says that he tried to use the enlisted man's practice of "not worrying about the future." He felt that he would be missed on shipboard at eight o'clock muster and that search planes would be sent out to look for him, since he was on a warship which was steaming far off the courses of any regular liners.

Bill Toles had such control of himself that he even tried to sleep by resting his head against a leg of the inflated dungarees, but the big waves kept slapping him awake. Controlling his fears, this young Navy man called upon his faith in "that something"—the power of God within him—and started repeating, over and over: *"Please, God—let me be rescued. . . . Please, God—let me be rescued . . . !"*

But when morning came and went and no planes appeared, Bill's spirits began to sink. He had become seasick from being flailed by the waves and swallowing so much water. Yet he never lost faith and kept repeating his prayer: *"Please, God—let me be rescued. . . . Please, God—let me be rescued . . . !"*

At three that afternoon, after Bill Toles had been in the water eleven hours, he was sighted by sailors on the *Executor,* an American Export Lines freighter, who were amazed to discover a man in the ocean!

But, even more amazing . . . the captain of this freighter could not explain why he had switched his ship from its usual course off Africa to a Spanish course which intersected the Navy carrier's homebound route!

Had he not done so, he would not have passed within several hundred miles of the *one little spot* in the vast ocean where Bill Toles, with his unfaltering faith in God, was awaiting rescue!

Bill was in such good physical shape, after all he had gone through, that he climbed the ship's ladder of the

Executor unassisted, and was toasted in champagne by the ship's crew.

But Bill Toles' first act was to thank God for answering his prayer.

Will you ever again doubt in the face of such evidence that "all things are possible to him that believeth"?

What *moved* that captain to change the course of his ship and go unerringly to this tiny spot in the millions of square miles of water, so he could pick up a man who had faith that God would let him be rescued?

There is no limit to the reach of mind and spirit! How strong is your faith? It should be a great deal stronger after this. You will probably never be called upon to exercise such faith, under such testing, emergency conditions. It should therefore be easier for you to know and believe and to say "it is so," with respect to whatever you need in life.

Your ship will find you, one of these days, laden with all you desire, if you hold on to your faith.

This *faith* must be positive, expectant, unwavering and utterly sincere or it will not energize "that something," the creative power within, which must be activated before what you have pictured can be attracted to you.

In an emergency, don't try to compel the answer to come to you at any specific time, because the God consciousness does not operate within the time limitations of earth. Setting a time limit will make you tense and cause you to doubt that you will receive help in time.

All you have to do is to maintain the faith that help will come to you at the time you need it most. Such an attitude of mind will free the God-given creative power of any and all self-imposed limitations and enable it to provide you with the aid and direction you must have to meet your particular crisis.

Bill Toles didn't question that God knew His business when he kept repeating, with faith, "Please God—let me be rescued." He *knew*—he *believed*—and so it was!

Cast aside your doubts forever because:

If you believe it—it's so!

12

I WILL—I WILL—I WILL—I WILL!

If you haven't the desire, by this time, to improve your own individual position in life, you had better stop reading right now and burn this. But if you are fired with new resolution to get somewhere—then I can assure you that you are on your way to progress.

Some types of individuals will read a book like this (as they have read *The Magic of Believing* and similar books) with mental chips on their shoulders. Many of them have had a smattering of every kind of *ism;* they have delved into occult subjects, Hindu philosophies; they have tried to spiritualize through faddish diets, all forms of self-denial, sublimation of sex, and so on; they have exposed themselves to "practical psychology," Unity, Astrology. They know all there is to be known, and still nothing has helped them.

Such people write in to say, not without some bitterness: "I have had very little results from my study of metaphysics, through no fault of mine, for I am conceded to be a good student, an intelligent person, and I understand the principles of metaphysics perfectly. I am very sorry to report, and so disappointed, too, that I am not getting any results from the methods outlined in your book. . . ."

Now these are no words of mine; this is a direct quotation from one of a number of letters I have received from well-meaning men and women who have gone from one book and religion and philosophy and *ism* and metaphysical practice to another, sampling here and sampling there, to prove to themselves that nothing will work for them! They want help desperately, but their mental and emotional attitude is such that they won't let themselves receive help. They are intellectually superior to everything they study; they are telling themselves "this won't work for me" even while they are reading about a suggestion or a technique of thinking that has accomplished wonders for thousands of others. These people are the perfectionists who are looking for the faults, the inconsistencies, the fallacies in everything, rather than for constructive and confirming points of agreement which can be applied to the solving of problems and correcting of unhappy conditions in their own lives. Subconsciously, something has happened to these men and women which has caused them to want to remain "problem children" to themselves and others. It is a way of getting attention, indulging their self-pity, getting even with a parent or someone else whom they feel has not treated them right or done enough for them. To salve their conscience for their inability to meet life as they should, they keep on studying metaphysics so they can continue to prove that they can't be helped "no matter how much they try."

One woman of this type confessed to me: "I've been

dealt one severe blow after another. I have always strived constantly to improve conditions in my life through metaphysics and prayer but without success. I can get conditions to start changing for the better and it will appear as though things are going to come right for me and that I will have happiness, but something always happens and my life pattern swings around back into the same old tragic, monotonous, nonsensical way, only it's worse each time. By now trouble, tragedy, unhappiness and loneliness have gotten to be a *fixed idea* in my consciousness, which I cannot break, try as I may!"

Of course it is difficult to see ourselves as others see us, to get an outside perspective, an impersonal evaluation of what we are doing to ourselves through our wrong thinking, that has been contributing to the unhappy conditions we continue to attract.

This same woman went on to say to me, "It's not true, your statement that 'a person should always do something for the other fellow, for it pays dividends.' Since a child, I have been doing good deeds for others but no one has ever done anything for me. People have come into my life under the guise of friends, accepting and taking advantage of my hospitality and generosity. Practically all of these so-called friends turned out to be merely spongers and bums. There is far more truth in the old saying, 'People will ride a free horse to death' than in the Bible verse, 'Cast your bread on the waters, and after many days it shall return unto you.' I have been casting my bread on the waters all my life and it has not returned to me yet. Evidently someone else grabs it before it gets back to me."

Do you detect that "mental chip" on her shoulder?

You cannot do a calculated good deed for another person, expecting something in return. This is not free-spirited giving. Nor can you help others who do not want help. They will resent it, and rightfully. When people insist on being nice to you, for no apparent reason, it makes you suspicious. You say to yourself, "Why are they going out of their way to do these things? Why are they trying to place me under obligation? What are they getting ready to request of me in exchange?"

You've heard many men and women say, "After all I've done for so-and-so, can you imagine this person treating me the way he has?"

There are times when friends and relatives selfishly or designedly take advantage of us, but there are also times when we mistakenly expect too much, when we get paid back in the kind of coin we give out.

This woman, and many like her, subconsciously "expects the worst while hoping for the best," and of course the worst always happens eventually, because this is the strongest, most emotionalized thought in her mind. She keeps herself magnetized, not to good, but to bad conditions, and thereby causes "that something," the creative power within, to produce a perpetuation of the unhappy experiences of her past. She expects people to be inconsiderate, to take advantage of her, to extend no help in time of need—and she works the creative law of life infallibly against herself. She is even picturing "someone grabbing the bread she has cast upon the waters before it gets back to her."

Isn't this an "inspired" sample of visualization? What can anyone expect from such mental picturing? Certainly not a loaf of bread, not even a crumb!

You who have gained an understanding of how mind functions, can see that this unhappy woman is a classic example of one who is operating the power successfully—in *reverse!*

There is one great, underlying fallacy in the thinking of these types of people. If they could only realize it, they could free themselves from their erroneous, fixed ideas and snap out of their difficulties in a hurry. Here it is:

People who claim they have never been able to make their higher powers of mind work for them have, on the contrary, through wrong *thinking, forced these very powers to work against them. They have caused these powers to produce failure instead of success, misery instead of happiness.*

Are you using the power within against yourself?

Ask yourself now, frankly and honestly, have you been doing this, in whole or in part? If you have, this is the root of your trouble. You haven't wanted to admit you have been misusing your life forces, your higher powers of mind. But there is only one power in you, and you must use it either for good or for ill, as the result of every thought you think, every emotionalized picture you place in consciousness!

Change your thinking and you instantly commence to change conditions around you. Change the direction of a magnet and it changes the field around it, immediately, automatically. But if you vacillate back and forth from good to bad, you lose what you have gained and produce an unsettled, unhappy result. You must hold your magnetization on what you want until it has been received. This requires an exercise of *will*, a developed determination, a resolution to "follow through," to stay with your constructive thinking, your right mental picturing for as long as is necessary to enable "that something," the creative power within, to help you reach your objective.

I will–I will–I will–I will!

Say this to yourself, again and again, and mean it! Look in the mirror and say it. Write it down and say it. Speak it out loud to yourself when you are going about your day's activities: "I will! I will! I will! I will!" Make this resolution a part of your consciousness, build up such a strength of determination within that nothing can shake it.

A colored man, one day, was trying to get a balky mule to move. You've probably heard the story. His boss came along and said, "George, why don't you try your will power on that jackass?" George shook his head. "I done tried it—but it don't do no good. He's usin' his *won't* power!"

Are you using your *won't* power? Are you telling yourself, deep down underneath, that owing to past failures, it won't be any use to try? If you are, you are killing off your will power at the very start. You can't say to yourself, on the surface, "I will" when something in your inner mind is saying right back to you, "But you can't. . . . You won't!"

The hardest people in this world to help are those who tell you at the very outset: "I can't. . . . I won't!"

"Won't power" is simply will power in reverse! You can get results from both, because they'll each serve you infallibly, as you call upon them. But "won't power" can bring you nothing, and will power can bring you everything. So why not choose your will power? Why stubbornly cling to your "won't power" because, perhaps, you don't really want to make the effort that will be required to help yourself; because you lack the faith in yourself and in the power within you should have; because you are afraid of trying and failing once more? You've got to start some time if you ever hope to make anything more of yourself than you are now. Are you satisfied with yourself as you exist at the present moment? Do you think the world owes you a living, that others should help you whether you try to help yourself or not, that if you hold on long enough and suffer long enough, a change for the better is going to come, anyway?

Don't kid yourself! There is only one way out of trouble and *you* have to lead the way. No one else can lead you or push you. Others can show you the way, set you on your feet and point you in the right direction, but you've got to do the *walking.*

I will–I will–I will–I will!

This *does* it! "I will" puts steam in your boilers, blows the top off inertia, starts sluggish brain cells in motion, puts new life and drive into body and mind.

"I won't" paralyzes initiative, incentive, enthusiasm; it stops everything from functioning, congests body and mind, and takes all the zest and purpose out of living.

Inject yourself with "I will" power!

Step right up, brother! Which do you want—an injection of "I will power" or "I won't power"?

This is the most important decision you can ever make. Your whole future depends upon it.

The first injection will bring you a greater measure of happiness, success and health than you have ever realized before.

The second injection will bring you a greater measure of misery, failure and ill health.

Take your choice! It's free! It doesn't cost anything. Both powers are equally available and equally reliable. They will work the moment you put them into operation by saying, "I will" or "I won't."

It is inconceivable that you will accept a further injection of "I won't!"—but you might, if you still hold hatred and resentment in your mind and heart, if you are sore at the world or at society and still want to prove that no power in heaven or on earth can or will help you!

A fixed idea is not easy to blast out of consciousness, but "I will" is the *power* that can do it! If you have gotten into the habit of "enjoying the worst," this habit will resist eviction to the last! You'll have to be hardboiled, ruthless with yourself and your past faults and weaknesses. Don't let self-pity take possession of you or any self-defensive feelings. If you do, "I can't" and "I won't" will remain in control. They will oppose "I will!" as long as they can, because they know they're through when "I will" moves in!

How about it? Have you joined the ranks of the "*I will*-ers?" If you have, don't ever again look back upon your "I won't" days. You have a new, ever-widening road ahead, filled with eager, joyous, progressing individuals who have added, "I can" to "I will," and are reaching objectives in their lives they never dared dream of before!

Say to yourself right now: "I will! I will! I will! I will!" Doesn't it *do* something to you—inside? Doesn't it lift your spirits, give you new hope, new ambition, new determination, new self-confidence?

Say, "I will!" and *believe* it—and you are on your way out of all past difficulties—forever!

13

POSITIVE THINKING CAN DISPEL FEAR AND WORRY

All of us are prone to calculate and weigh things, permitting the negative side to creep to the fore, and our thoughts evidence themselves in such remarks as *"It can't be done"*; *"I'm afraid"*; *"What will happen if I do it?"* *"People won't understand"*; *"It isn't worth the effort"*; *"I haven't the time"* and similar verbal alibis. If you haven't expressed these thoughts to yourself, then others have to you, and, through the power of suggestion, you have accepted them as your own conclusions.

It takes an affirmative type to make progress, and you should know, by now, how to develop yourself into the affirmative type.

The negative type is sunk before he starts. Nature takes care of these situations through the old law of the survival of the fittest. We know what happened in the days of ancient Sparta when children were put on their own as babies, and only those who survived were given further chance.

A negative type is a quitter; or, putting it another way, a quitter is a negative type. There is no point to going around hitting everybody on the nose, just to start something. Just the same, it's poor business to let yourself be put on the defensive in everything you attempt to do in life, as that is a negative sign.

The person who won't be licked, can't be licked.

If you are taken unawares and suddenly put on the defensive, snap out of it. Take the offensive as soon as you can, because if you remain on the defensive, you are beaten.

One of your greatest enemies in life will always be *fear*. This is what makes many people negative, what keeps them from assuming and maintaining a positive attitude. Fear is the Great Destroyer. Give fear command of your life and you will be powerless to achieve anything worth while.

Some 3,500 years ago, Job said:

For the thing which I greatly feared is come upon me, and that which I was afraid of is come unto me.

Certainly they came upon him because he, in his fears, pictured these things . . . he used the immutable law to attract them. Just as you bring the *good* things which you want into reality by holding the positive thoughts constant, so do you bring the *bad* things—those which you fear—by holding the worry, the negative thoughts constant.

If you have read this far, then you must realize that when you look after your thoughts, your thoughts will look after you! This being true, which will it be—grief, trouble, ill health, worry, failure—or health, wealth, happiness, success? It's entirely up to you. No power on this earth but you can direct your thoughts, and the way you use your will to keep your thoughts positive is a matter solely under your control.

Our late President Franklin Delano Roosevelt made one terrific statement when he said: *"The only thing we have to fear is fear itself!"*

He knew whereof he spoke, and millions of people who heard him make this statement knew that he knew because they had only to check the effect of fear in thei. own lives to realize that fear itself was even worse than the things feared!

It is often easier to face something you have feared than it is to anticipate the facing of it, because your imagination usually exaggerates, through fear, what you are afraid may happen to you.

Many people are ashamed when they finally meet a situation they had feared, only to find it isn't nearly as bad or difficult as they had thought it would be.

Eliminate your fear pictures

You should always remember that since you think in pictures, every wrong picture which enters your consciousness, with intense feelings of fear behind it, is like a seed which takes root in mind and, eventually, reproduces similiar happenings in your life.

To protect yourself from the increasing effect of wrong emotional reactions, or your occurring and recurring fears, you must acquire the ability to control your feelings. You are still, more or less, a victim of fear and worry if you catch yourself expressing your feelings and apprehensions like this:

"I'm so worried, I can't think straight."

"I've a feeling that nothing I try to do will turn out right."

"I've lost faith in myself—and in God."

"I'm so nervous and tense, I haven't slept for weeks."

"I can't get over what happened to me."

"I know better but I can't help burning myself up with hate and resentment and fear."

"I've lost all interest in living—I'd put myself out of the way if I weren't afraid to do it."

"The doctor says if I don't learn to control my fears and worries, I'll kill myself."

Does this sound like you or like remarks you have made? If it does, it's time you were getting busy and eliminating this negative, defeatist attitude.

Thousands of men and women have either written me or told me that fear and worry have them down, that they can't rise above these feelings. They'd like to have me wave a wand over them, say "Abracadabra" and chase their fears and worries away. This would be much easier than going to work on themselves, applying the knowledge I have given them and am giving them in this book. But I have had to tell them in all frankness, straight from the shoulder, "Much as I would like to be of further help to you—the law doesn't work that way. As long as you do nothing but complain of these conditions which you have brought upon yourself through *fear thinking*, these unhappy conditions are due to continue."

This isn't good news to many; but it serves to shock a certain percentage into action. It depends upon how deeply you really *want* to rid yourself of the plague of fears and worries. You can't do it without exercising your will, without changing your thoughts from negative to positive! And this doesn't mean being positive one minute and negative the next.

You must keep at it!

I'm amused at these people who tell me they are "holding the right thought." I ask them, "For how long?" and they say, "Well, for a few minutes, anyway." You've got to get yourself in hand so that you can *live* the right thought, not for a few minutes, but day after day.

How far would you get in a tennis game if you returned a few balls hit by your opponent, then went to the sidelines and sat down for a few minutes, then got up and started playing again and returned a few more balls, and went back and sat down? It would be pretty silly, wouldn't it?

Well, the game of life is being played all the time . . . and to win it, you've got to stay in the game, whether you like it or not. You've got to return everything that's hit at you, with all the power you can put on the ball. Your opponent is fear and worry. The only way to defeat him is by *taking positive, aggressive action.* Stop trying to run away. Stand up to fear and worry. Look your enemies in the eye, make them back down and do a fade-out. When you face fear with courage, fear takes it on the lam. Fear is through, he's whipped, he has no power over you as soon as you throw him a fast one with "Courage" and "I will!" written on it. This is the pulverizer. You can't be positive and negative at the same time, one or the other must prevail. Your head may be bloody but as long as you don't bow it, as long as you remain undaunted and unafraid, you will have your old enemy fear routed. He can't retain any hold on you under these positive conditions.

There's an old saying, "You don't get ulcers from what you eat—you get them from what's eating *you!*"

Fear can upset the chemistry of your body and make you susceptible to all manner of illnesses. Fear causes heart palpitation, indigestion, shortness of breath, nervous perspiration, nerve tension, allergic reactions and a host of other physical reactions which, in time, develop into more serious disturbances.

"I'm afraid of the dark, afraid of falling, afraid of fire, afraid of this and that, in fact I'm just about afraid of everything!" some people tell me.

"Well, what are you doing about it?" I ask them.

"What *can* I do?" many reply. "I'm just afraid, that's all!"

Afraid, afraid. Repetition . . . repetition . . . the more they fear, the *more* they fear! Like always attracts like! A snowball starts rolling down a snow-covered hill. It's a little snowball at the beginning and it's an avalanche at the bottom. Unless you break up the snowball of fear it will engulf and submerge you.

Give your fears a chance to grow, keep on nourishing them with more fears and you'll have a tidal wave to contend with before you're through.

Worry, of course, is the handmaiden of fear. I was going to say she is the "consort."

George Washington Lyon has said: *"Worry is the interest paid by those who borrow trouble."*

John Bunyan said he was able to eliminate worry from two days of each week. He wrote:

There are two days in the week about which and upon which I never worry. Two carefree days, kept sacredly free from fear and apprehension. One of these days is yesterday ... And the other is tomorrow!

Now, if you can eliminate fear and worry from yesterday and tomorrow, you have only to eliminate it from *today,* and you have it licked!

Ah! but today is the only time you are alive. Today is the only time you have to face reality. Today is the only time you have to *do* anything, constructive or destructive. Today, before it becomes *yesterday,* is your opportunity to go forward or backward! Today, before it becomes *tomorrow* is your chance to lay a better foundation for your future!

What are you doing with today? Are you filling it full of your usual fears and worries, thus guaranteeing that tomorrow will be a repetition of today?

Positive and negative thought
Rules the world, for good or ill

Any downward or upward trend in our world-wide economic scheme is due entirely to the way we think. When the great world leaders, the statesmen, the financiers, editors, publishers, economists, those who direct and influence the thoughts of millions in every part of the globe, permit depressed thoughts to enter into their scheme, then depressed thoughts and fear vibrations enter into the scheme of those same millions and business comes to a near standstill.

When the world's leaders change their way of thinking, toss out fear and move forward instead of backwards, then the thoughts of millions change for the better and as they think constructively, business improves.

Fear, the plague of humanity, must be overcome!

Today the world is fear-ridden. The threat of A-bombs and H-bombs, and who knows what other kinds of new and even more destructive bombs, hangs over the globe. Under such horrific conditions, it is no wonder that the economic life of millions in all lands is in a delicate state of unbalance, and that fear of a third world war exists in the minds of great masses of people. Add to this the profound hates and resentments which seethe among various races, the fears and suspicions which, unhappily, tragically exist, and it requires great faith and courage for the individual to maintain the right mental attitude.

But, in the face of all this, it is absolutely imperative that you learn to control your emotions—your fears and worries—that you *picture* yourself receiving guidance and protection from the power within, so that you will be safe and secure, no matter what may come to pass in the world at large, so that you can do all in your power to help bring about better conditions in your community and extend your own influence for good as far as possible.

Be positive! Be courageous, believe, have faith, prepare your mind today, so that you can to a great degree control your individual future.

Remember this: human beings are human beings the world over, whether in Prague or Timbuctoo; all subject to the same emotions, the same influences, the same vibrations; and what is a community, a city, a nation but merely a collection of individual human beings?

Once again: *"As a man thinketh in his heart so is he."*

As members of a community think—so they are; as a city thinks—so is it, and as a nation thinks—so is it! Make your contribution to the thought of your times where you live. Your positive attitude will help others become more positive. Never mind a few setbacks . . . or obstructions.

When a train roars across the track in front of you, you put on the brakes of your automobile, throw the gears into neutral and idle your engine. You are on your way again just as soon as the train passes but you certainly do not throw your gears into reverse and go *backwards!*

Compare yourself to the gears of your automobile. In *reverse,* place all fears, worries, troubles, aches and pains. Okay. Then when things go wrong, intead of getting upset about it, losing control of yourself, simply put on the brakes, idle your engine until you can clearly see the road ahead.

In high is everything you desire: health, wealth, happiness, success. No power in the world except your hand can put the gears of your automobile in reverse. If your own gears get in reverse, remember: *You alone* put them there! And you put them there with your own thoughts, because:

"There is nothing either good or bad, but thinking makes it so."

Hamlet—Act. II, Sc. 2

Therefore, as you think, you move either forward or backward, in high gear or in reverse. When you place

159

yourself in reverse, worry and fret, you are using the *tap, tap* idea to bring into existence the things you would most avoid!

Say to yourself: "From this moment on I will be positive!" When you say it, mean it!

Erect a steel wall on the right side of the reverse gear so that you will never go into reverse again. Close the door of yesterday. Keep it closed. Then shift from low gear to high—and *stay* there!

14

AMAZING EVIDENCE OF THOUGHT
TRANSFERENCE

Before you can accomplish what you want to achieve, in
and through your own mind, you must know more about
the workings of your subconscious. There is a great deal
of mystery associated with its functioning, and many scientists, physicians, biologists, anthropologists, psychologists, physicians, psychiatrists and every other kind of
authority are trying to gain more light on what happens
in the deep recesses of man's brain. They've now discovered that great sections of a man's brain can be removed without impairing his consciousness or his
intelligence. You've heard of the electroencephalograph,
that sensitized apparatus that detects and records brain
waves. I've recently learned of a new instrument, now
under development, by which the positive and negative
currents in every organ of the body can be charted, to
determine their "electrical" state of health.

You see, the physical body isn't the grossly material

organism we once thought it was. It is now referred to as an electro-chemical machine of great sensitivity. A few years ago, scientists thought that the so-called "soul" was a part of the body, and died with the body. Today, they are not so sure. In fact, many scientists have concluded that intelligence, consciousnes, may not be a part of the body at all, but simply manifests *through* the body. Picture yourself, then, as a temporary tenant, living in your wonderful house of flesh, gaining experience and evolving your soul or consciousness through this experience while here, finally departing from this house when it has become impaired or outworn its usefulness.

Fantastic? Nothing is fantastic any more in this Buck Rogers age. What the mind of man can conceive, the mind of man can achieve. Man has desired immortality for as long as man has had conscious existence. He has dreamed and written and sung of a "life to come" in his religions, his philosophies, his songs and his personal aspirations. Now it is becoming apparent that man has been intuitively sensing "a land beyond the reach of the five physical senses," no less real than the world he is now in, a land which awaits his coming after the change called "death."

As you develop your own awareness, you, too, will become conscious of an increasingly positive conviction that "this life is not all"; that it is "just the beginning" of a continuously unfolding experience and adventure in God's great universe!

The key to this deeper understanding of self and your true relationship to the God consciousness within is to be found in your developed control and direction of the subconscious part of you.

How much do you know about your subconscious mind? Do you know it's the most remarkable mechanism in the universe? Perhaps "mechanism" isn't the right word: but you've got to call it something. It operates with the precision of a watch *if* you properly direct it. If you had a servant who trusted you implicitly and followed your every order right down to the minutest detail, brought you everything you thought you wanted, whether it was good or bad for you—you would have a small sample of what your subconscious does.

It stores away for your future use all the mental pictures and feelings of experiences you have had. How you feel about anybody or anything is filed in your subconscious. Your fears and worries and hates and prejudices are all there . . . along with your good thoughts. When you think good thoughts, you tune in on other good thoughts of the same nature that are already on file. If you like somebody today and nothing happens to change this regard, you will like him more tomorrow, because each day's feelings about that person is added to the feelings of day before. Repetition is a tremendous force.

Start doing things a certain way, and you'll keep on doing them that way unless you change your mind or something happens to make you act differently. You form a groove in your mind like the groove in a phonograph record—but the groove doesn't have to stay that way. You can make a new groove any time you wish, because you are a creature of free will and free choice and your subconscious mind is always controlled and directed by your conscious desires and decisions.

Your subconscious is a vast reservoir of knowledge

which you have acquired through past experience and education and reflective thinking. It also possesses knowledge that it brings to you through your intuitive faculties, your extrasensory organs, because a part of your subconscious is not limited by time or space. It is a powerhouse of energy which reaches out into the universe around you and brings you an awareness of things that could never get through your conscious mind alone. Just how your subconscious does all this no one knows, but scientists are gathering plenty of proof that you are a powerful sending and receiving station with what amounts to a universal hookup. You can be put in contact with just about anybody or anything you want. Of course, not many of us are developed to the point that we can direct these higher powers so as to communicate *consciously* with the physical, mental, psychic and, according to many investigators, spiritual worlds, past, present and future ... but we are told this will, one day, be possible!

Your body is a reflector of your thought!

Your subconscious is the one part of you that never sleeps. If it ever lay down on the job your body would stop functioning, for it contains that miraculous intelligence which keeps your heart beating, your lungs breathing, your stomach digesting whatever you eat (and don't think that doesn't take some real doing, at times!). Every organ of your body, including the functioning of your five physical senses, is regulated by your subconscious, and if you don't interfere with its control by throwing a monkey wrench into your subconscious machinery in the form of fear or worry, your heart never skips a beat, you breathe without thinking about it, and you never know that your stomach is digesting your food. But start getting upset about something, making your body tense—and watch your heart start to palpitate, notice how your breath gets short, and you don't feel like eating because your stomach is tied in a knot. Maybe you even get sick at your stomach. This ought to teach you to take care of your thinking and let your subconscious take care of your body. If you tell your subconscious that you are upset, your subconscious has to tell your body the same thing, because your body—the house you live in—is just a reflection of your thought. You can't say that you feel bad, and feel good.

Give your subconscious mind a problem to work on just before you go to sleep. Have faith that this higher intelligence within you can and will solve this problem. Forget about it, and in the morning, as like as not, you'll wake up with the answer or know what to do to get the answer. The more you practice giving your subconscious jobs to do, the more it will carry the ball for you. It's the most willing servant you will ever have! It doesn't mind how much you pile on the work, how many problems you hand it, how many desires or goals you are carrying in consciousness at one time. Remember: your subconscious is not limited in its operation, except as you limit it by your limited thinking.

This amazing subconscious possesses a power that, for want of any better way to describe it, is magnetic. It seems to magnetize conditions around you the moment you give it a clear picture of what you desire. And it commences attracting everything you need, even the people you need to meet, to help you get what you are after.

Things start happening so naturally that you often don't realize your subconscious mind is doing it for you. It is using all of its powers—on the physical, mental and spiritual levels of your life—and focusing these powers on your objective.

You can't fail if you properly instruct your subconscious and maintain your faith in the wonder-working God Power within. But the most mysterious of all your subconscious workings is what science calls its "extra-sensory faculties."

What you need to know about extra-sensory perception!

Your are familiar, I suppose, with the exhaustive experiments along parapsychological lines which Dr. J. B. Rhine and his staff at Duke University have conducted and are still carrying out. A little briefing on his work will be of value.

Dr. Rhine undertook his experiments, years ago, on the theory that the human mind can become aware of facts or conditions, at varying or unlimited distances from the body, with or without the agency of another mind in transmission and receiving. He began his experiments with cards of his devising, containing the heavy, black symbols of a cross, a circle, a square, a triangle, and a wavy line. His subjects were required to sit in different rooms or buildings, and attempt to transmit and receive impressions of these symbols. Others sought to get impressions of the order of these symbols in a deck by concentration upon the deck, without any other human mind knowing the order in advance. Still others sought to record their impressions of the order that these cards would fall in when they would be shuffled at some future moment in time, to see if it was possible for the mind to foretell the coming of a specific event or happening.

All of these experiments, repeated laboriously and painstakingly, with every precaution taken against possible conscious or unconscious fraud, suggestion or physical causation, have produced quantitatively and positively results that were definitely above and beyond chance.

There is no longer any scientific doubt that these higher powers of mind exist. In fact, the influence of mind upon animals and plants and inanimate objects has also been demonstrated. And still we aren't even out of the kindergarten with respect to the knowledge of consciousness and its fundamental relationship to the world within and without ourselves, which will one day be revealed.

There are thousands upon thousands of authentic, well-witnessed cases of men and women and children who have received impressions either of a telepathic, clairvoyant or precognitive nature. These impressions have come to them in the form of mental pictures, strong feelings or knowing sensations, in the waking or dream state. They have sensed or "seen" happenings to friends and loved ones, or even strangers, taking place at a distance from them, or still to take place in some future moment of time. Under certain established conditions of receptivity and concentration, mind can communicate with mind, unobstructed by such supposed barriers as time and space.

You can develop similar powers of mind

But it has already been pointed out that your sub-conscious mind, and the powers it possesses, is not limited by time and space. When you have learned how to control your own mind and emotions, you, too, can transmit and receive thoughts.

Should you wish to attempt any telepathic experiments of your own, there is a definite pattern to follow. Many men and women have tried it and have reported their amazement at the correct impressions they have received. First, relax your physical body from head to foot, letting go of it completely with your conscious mind. This in itself is not easy, but it can be acquired with practice. Then, having made your conscious mind passive (divesting it of all thoughts) *look within your mind,* figuratively turning your physical eyesight *inward,* focusing it upon what I call a "mental-picture screen." This is an imaginary white screen which hangs in the darkness of inner consciousness, and on which, on the principle of television, is flashed the images that hit the mind from the outside source.

It is my conviction that we all possess these higher sensory powers in dormant or partially developed form and that when we give recognition to them—when we have faith that these powers can and will serve us—they commence to function for us! Doubt and disbelief keep these powers from manifesting just as definitely as doubt and disbelief prevent your creative powers of mind from operating in and through you. These extra-sensory faculties are all part of the same great power. When you get a sudden, unexplainable impulse or urge to do or not to do, this is your intuition. These extra-sensory perceptions are trying to deliver a message to you.

Occasionally you will receive an impression or a mental picture flash of a future event, some happening that is coming toward you in time. Don't let your conscious mind argue you out of it if you get a strong feeling of conviction that this premonitory impression is genuine.

I believe that man has it in his power to create, to a very large degree, his own future, his own destiny. The more he can learn to develop and depend upon his higher powers of mind, his intuitive faculties, and follow his genuine hunches and premonitions, the more he can avoid unhappy experiences and attract good happenings to him.

While I have devoted years to such development as I have attained, almost everyone at some time in his life can testify to an experience when his mind tuned in on the thoughts of another. I am indebted to Mrs. J. R. Hutchinson of LaJolla, California, for this outstanding illustration:

"When my daughter was about three years old, possibly four, which would have been in 1925, I attended a party one night. The favors were little paper Japanese parasols. I told my friends at the party that I was going to take my parasol home to my daughter and they gave me their parasols to give to her, too. She loved them and played with them for a long, long time, during which time I found a cute little song about a 'paper parasol' and she and I used to sing it together. Since then, I don't recall having thought of the words or the tune.

"On the morning of June 10th, this year, I arose with a haunting little tune which kept recurring in my mind. Finally the words came, one by one, and after a couple of hours, during which I went about my household duties, the whole song came back to me, words and music. My husband was working out in the garden and I rushed out to him and asked if he'd like to hear a cunning little song about 'the little paper parasol.' I sang it to him, over and over, and told him how it had been running through my mind all morning. He is a very matter-of-fact person and laughed good-humoredly at me for making such a fuss about it. Then I forgot the whole incident.

"On June 18th, I found in our mailbox an envelope from Mexico which appeared to have more than just sheets of paper inside. I carried it into the house, wondering who it could be from and what it could contain, how it got past the import people, and so on. When I opened it—there, to my surprise—was a *little paper parasol*—and a note, from my daughter, saying: '*Remember the little girl to whom you brought tiny Japanese umbrellas after you went to grown-up parties?*'

"Unfortunately, there was no date on my daughter's message and because of the way the stamp was cancelled, I could not see the exact date of mailing. But I had, of course, not written my daughter about singing the little song previously, or thinking so strongly of the little parasol. Just the same—it's very evident to me that she picked up my thoughts or I picked up hers. After all these years, anything as unusual as this could not have been a coincidence!"

Of course it couldn't have been a coincidence! Mind communicates with mind, between friends and loved ones particularly, much more often than we consciously realize!

There are those who believe that they can communicate, on occasion, with dear ones who have gone on, through mind. Why not? If human beings survive death and can communicate, mind to mind, while on earth, they should still be able to reach us through mind when we have developed our powers of sensitivity highly enough ... or in our dreams, when the conscious mind is blanked out and we are in the subconscious realm, not bounded by time or space!

Arthur Godfrey, in an issue of that fine little inspirational magazine, *Guideposts,* tells of a "psychic experience" of his own:

"It was in 1923. I was stationed on board a Navy destroyer—in charge of radio communications. I had knocked around a lot since I had left home. The years and life had not been too kind but the Navy had been a sanctuary, the only security I had known for a long time. One day, I fell asleep in my bunk and dreamed.

"My Dad—I had not seen him for years—suddenly walked into the room. He offered his hand, saying, 'So long, kid!' I answered, 'So long, Dad.' I said some kind of prayer. It wasn't eloquent but it came from the heart.

"I never saw him again. When I woke up, my buddies told me that at the exact time while I was asleep, the wires from shore hummed the news of my Dad's death.

"Don't tell me about science and its exact explanation of everything. Some things are bigger. God is the difference. He gets around."

Yes, God *is* the difference ... the God Power within. But it's up to you to develop this power and learn to use it in your every-day life. Train yourself to follow your hunches, the guidance you receive from the impressions that come to you. If you believe in your higher powers, if you have faith they will operate for you, they will! And once you have had any experiences of your own, similar to those described in this chapter, you will never doubt again!

15

YOUR MIND CAN PERFORM
HEALINGS

To lick the world, it's necessary to be in good health! You need vitality of body to support an energetic m_nd. Those who have to carry sick and ailing bodies around with them are often laboring under self-imposed handicaps. In many instances, their own wrong thinking and emotional reactions have brought the illnesses upon them.

Cross-examine yourself! If you don't possess the degree of health you should have, what have you been doing to help create these disturbed conditions? You can be sure you've been doing something to upset the chemistry of your body by letting some fears, worries, hates or resentments run riot inside you. Nothing happens by accident. There are causes behind even the most insignificant things that occur. It's now an established fact that your body reflects the attitudes of your mind, if these attitudes become chronic. You well know that worry and apprehension can upset your digestion, cause your heart to palpitate, bring on a shortness of breath and nervous perspiration. A sudden fright can do all that. So don't try to tell me that how you think and feel doesn't affect your health!

Now, get this important point: if your mind has the power to make you sick, through wrong thinking, it obviously has the power to make you well, to heal you, through right thinking!

I do not claim that the power of will, the creative power, is a cure-all; but I do know that the right mental attitude will aid any person in ill health. Do you remember the Frenchman, Dr. Émile Coué, who was in this country some years ago, telling people they could cure themselves if they would adopt his plan? His idea was very simple. All you had to do was say to yourself, over and over: *"Every day, in every way, I am getting better and better."*

Lots of folks laughed at Dr. Coué. His method was so simple that they said he was "nuts." There was nothing new in his idea, any more than there is anything new in the ideas I'm putting forth. Just another way of expressing the whole scheme . . . reiteration, repetition . . . keeping uppermost in mind all the time what you want. . . . Those positive thoughts, in turn, are passed on to the subconscious mind—the creative power within.

Think health, wealth and happiness and they will all be yours, in time. It cannot be otherwise!

Hold on now! You can't be silly about this thing! Good ideas like Dr. Coué's have lost their value to many people because they have seen others going overboard.

You can't kid yourself by giving lip service to "Every day, in every way, I am getting better and better," when you are doing nothing to change wrong mental attitudes or habits or practices which have brought on ill health.

You can't "hold the right thought" and expect to get anywhere if you are full of a hundred "wrong thoughts."

We all know of people who are continually talking about backaches, headaches, stomach aches or some other kind of aches. They harp on them and the first thing they know, with that reiteration, the aches become realities. If you have such an ache or pain, if you've determined that it is nothing serious, just a nerve or tension reaction of some sort, there is no point in talking about it; neither is there any point to talking about your worries, your troubles. All this does is to further annoy yourself, and others. They have worries and troubles of their own they want to talk about, and they are apt to resent your beating them to the punch. And it's some punch, too; when you don't feel right, it hits you smack in the solar plexus. You go around with that hang-dog, all-gone feeling and the more you repeat how lousy you feel, the more certain you are that you should keep within reach of an undertaker. Constant reflection on your ills will magnify them and cement them to you.

Get away from the negative side and become an affirmative type. Think affirmatively, and the first thing you know, your aches, worries and troubles will disappear. They can't continue to live off you if you refuse to give them nourishment.

"If thou art pained by any external thing, it is not this thing which disturbs thee, but thy own judgment

about it. And it is in thy power to wipe out this judgment now. But if anything in thy own disposition gives thee pain, who hinders thee from correcting thy opinion?"

Philosophy of the Ages

The healing power of love

Scientists at Harvard, under the direction of Professor Pitirim A. Sorokin, are conducting a most unusual experiment. They are studying the *power of love.* They have already discovered that love has more power over disease than medicine. Right doses of this emotion can produce longer life, greater health and happiness, as well as peace of mind. Young and old are transformed when the love potion is taken. If you don't like somebody and have been burning yourself up hating him, start loving that person, and see what happens. You're apt to end up with a friend instead of an enemy, and a stomach free of ulcers. Most human beings never forget an insult, but they remember a kindness even longer. Since like attracts like, wouldn't you rather give out with love and kindness and get love and kindness back?

You've heard people say, "I'll get even with so-and-so if it takes the rest of my life!" Carrying such resentment around with them takes far more out of them than it does the person hated

Everyone wants to be loved, even a dog; and everyone warms up to love, even a dog. You feel better when you love and are loved. Look at the dried-up men and women around you who are starved for love, if you think love isn't a mighty, creative, vital force! Several scientists

have tried loving some plants and hating
plants that were nourished with love have
the plants poisoned by hate, but given the sa
ical care and watering, have been undersized or   en
shriveled up and died!

There's an old saying, "You can love a person to death"; but I'll take my chances any day on love against hate. Get the hate out of your life if you wish to attain and retain good health!

Your mind can heal you

There is a creative power in mind which, properly directed, can heal you. I have used this power to heal different physical disturbances which have developed in me through wrong thinking, and you can learn to use it, too.

One of my dear friends is Dr. Frederick Bailes, Director of the great Science of Mind Church in Los Angeles. He conducts a healing service each Sunday morning at the Fox-Wilshire Theatre, this includes a meditation period, which is worth crossing the country to experience. A capacity audience of twenty-five hundred people sit in absolute silence, calling upon this God-given creative power, "that something" within them. Each pictures whatever physical condition needs correction, in themselves or others, as restored to normal. Results always border on the astounding, and this is so because Dr. Bailes is a man who has practiced what he preaches. He has healed himself and he knows how to help others heal themselves. For this reason, I have asked Dr. Bailes to tell you of his own healing so that you can apply this same method to your specific needs. Here it is:

"In 1915 I was completing my training in London Missionary School of Medicine, connected with London Homeopathic Hospital, preparatory to going to Bolivia as a medical missionary. One month before graduation, I became ill; laboratory tests confirmed the diagnosis of diabetes, which was invariably fatal, especially in a younger person. The best physicians in Harley Street gave me a year or two to live.

"At this time I was steeped in the medical tradition, and would have used medical methods of treatment, but since this was five years before Banting's work with insulin, there was no medicinal drug which had any effect upon this condition.

"Two of the visiting physicians with whom I had worked in the hospital were beginning to delve into the interaction between mind and body. We had experimented with certain out-patients by the use of placebos, which were non-medicinal tablets made to look like medicine. In many instances we had found that the placebos produced as much improvement as the genuine drug might have been expected to produce. For example, we would tell the patient to take three pills daily for a week, then would have the dispensary issue only sufficient for five days, and all fifteen pills would be placebos. Frequently, the patient would say on his return, 'Doctor, I felt fine until Thursday, but my pills ran out, and I've suffered terribly the past two days.'

"Since some of these patients suffered from serious conditions, and since I had seen patients under hypnosis freed from extreme distress without the use of morphine, I decided that some sort of mental technique might work for me, especially if I would go into it with my eyes open, thus requiring no placebos.

"This I did! Since a myriad new cells were built every moment, and since each was built under the dominant idea either of health or of illness, I determined that I would stamp each new cell with the concept of health, right structure, right action, right function, and would begin to praise the body for its mutual co-operation and assistance, one part with the other.

"Fortunately, I was quite familiar with the internal structure of the pancreas, having dissected several of them, and I could have drawn a picture of the Islets of Langerhans which are the chemical laboratory in which Infinite Intelligence synthetizes insulin from its components. I began to talk to it, telling it that I knew it wanted to work, that it did not enjoy being on a sitdown strike, that something in my past mental and emotional attitudes had turned it aside from its will to work, and that from now on it would have all the co-operation it needed from me.

"One might ask, 'But did you really *believe* it could hear you?' Of course not! But the mere framing of the picture in this way did something to me. I was a child in metaphysics, and knew nothing of techniques; I was as alone as Robinson Crusoe in this new spiritual world, and this was the best way I could devise of to counterbalance whatever in me had caused the stoppage.

"Of one thing I was *certain,* that the *mental pic-*

ture could produce definite changes in the body. I had seen this already in the hospital. I was now coming to see that this universe is a universe of *pure thought*. I knew nothing then of the researches that such noted astrophysicists as Eddington and Jeans were then embarked upon, and which have done so much to prove that the universe is one big thought, clothed with form. But I firmly believed that each new cell could receive the impression of my recently oriented thought, so I used whatever words would help me actually to believe the words I was ostensibly saying to my body.

"The hospital experiments had demonstrated that thoughts and beliefs could definitely affect the body, sometimes in serious disorders. But as far as I knew, no one had ever been healed of so profound a malady as *diabetes*. However, when the alternative is death, a desperate person will try anything.

"I knew that nothing goes on in the universe without some previous action of intelligence. Action is preceded by mental activity. The universe is what Jeans calls 'the thought of the Mathematical Thinker, condensed into rigorous form.' Man's body could quite reasonably be to man what the universe is to the Infinite Thinker, the outpicturing of his individual thought. All thought being therefore creative, the nature and condition of that which is being created would depend on the nature and condition of the thought. I felt that I was on sound, reasonable, logical grounds in thus making the attempt to color this creative process in the direction of *perfect function*.

"For perhaps eight or ten weeks there was no

apparent change, but I persisted. Then, one week, the laboratory test showed a very slight drop in the sugar. Next week it fell further. Unfortunately, I kept no diary, therefore these periods might not be exactly correct; but my general recollection is that the sugar fell for several weeks. Then for no apparent reason, it soared again. This was most discouraging, but I continued with my procedures, and the sugar dropped again. This intermittent rise and fall of the sugar continued for almost six years, during which time I was steadily gaining a sense of mastery over the condition.

"The encouraging feature to me was that each peak of the flare-ups was never quite so high as the previous high point. Eventually, the day came when the urinalysis revealed the fact that the sugar had fallen to the point where it was no longer listed in a percentage figure, and the laboratory report merely said: 'Sugar, a trace.' But this trace persisted for probably six or eight months before the laboratory report said, 'Sugar, negative.' This was perhaps the happiest day of my life; yet I was cautious for some months, still refraining largely from carbohydrates in my diet.

"Gradually I came to the conviction that my trouble was gone, and by this time I had learned how to put a certain finality into my belief, so that I knew that never again would I be brought under bondage to this condition.

"For over thirty years I have eaten all the sugars and starches I have desired. I have never in my life had a drop of insulin. My energy and vitality are higher than that of most men of my age, and it has been my supreme pleasure to teach thousands

of others this creative principle which has brought
me out from under the shadow of death."

Doesn't this thrill you? The same creative power
resides in you this very minute, ready for you to call upon
it, to serve you, as the creative power in Dr. Bailes' consciousness served him. All you have to do is to start using
it, calling upon it, directing it, exercising your will, determination, persistence, visualization, faith!

If you believe it, it is so!

Read and reread Dr. Bailes' description of how he
did it; keeping in mind, the while, how *you* can apply
these methods in your own life!

But, don't be foolish about this thing. Remember
the little ever-true gem of wisdom, "Babies crawl before
they can walk." If you are a diabetic . . . don't jump off
the deep end before you can swim. Start preparing your
mind, freeing it of fears and worries and every kind of
emotional disturbance. Make contact with this God-given
creative power—this healing force. Experiment with it,
in little things. Observe how your body responds, how
your health improves, as you maintain happier, more joyous and confident attitudes of mind. Whatever mental
and emotional states you have had which helped bring
on this physical condition must be removed. As you do
this—you are bound to improve in general health. And
the power may then come to you to employ healing in
your life, as Dr. Bailes was able to demonstrate it in his.
Check your development, your progress, with your doctor. All physicians now admit the great aid that a right

mental attitude has in any physical recovery. They know that faith is a potent force, that when the twin killers, fear and worry are slain, the biggest job has been done!

NEVER give up hope. If physicians have passed the death sentence upon you—then you must place full dependence upon faith and the God-given healing power within you. Under these circumstances, it may be possible for you to so activate the cells of your body by your own right thinking, that a healing will take place. It has happened to thousands of other men and women when all hope was apparently gone; and what they have been able to do, you, too, can do!

We are beginning to comprehend the *potential* of this healing power we possess within us, not only as it can be utilized by us, but as we can apply it, to others, and even to the aid of our pets! Yes, whatever possesses intelligence can be reached by us—through *feeling*. You have a strong feeling of love for a dear one, and a different but equally strong feeling of love for a dog or a horse or a cat, or some other animal. Such feelings are often mutual. You can feel the love of a dear one for you . . . the love of a dog or a horse or a cat . . . whatever form of life with which you are in harmony.

An amazing case of healing!

As proof of this, I'm now going to present an almost incredible but well-authenticated account of how Ann Davies, another friend of mine, who understands and operates "that something," the creative power within, performed an instantaneous healing on her dog, Tzaddi!

Here is Ann's own story, which is supported by affidavits from the veterinarian and five witnesses of the phenomenon:

"Over two years ago, I first observed a tiny growth in the mouth of my dog, Tzaddi, which was about the size of a pea. I thought it was a wart, and since she didn't seem troubled, I was not too disturbed. However, from time to time, I examined her mouth, and about a year ago, I noticed that the growth was getting larger.

In June of 1952, the growth started to grow more rapidly, and I became worried, so I took Tzaddi to our veterinarian, for diagnosis. He examined Tzaddi's mouth, and told me that the growth was a tumor, and that mouth tumors are quite serious for they almost always become malignant, and recommended that I do not wait too long before surgery.

"Due to circumstances beyond my control, I was unable to return Tzaddi to the veterinarian until September 4, 1952, at which time the tumor had grown alarmingly, being about the size of half of my end thumb joint. Tzaddi was quite uncomfortable, and all my friends had been observing this with me.

"Dr. Short was alarmed over the rapid growth, and said we must operate immediately. An appointment was made for Saturday morning, September 6th, 8 A.M.

"I retired late, on Friday night of September 5th. In fact, it was really Saturday morning at 2 A.M. that I got into bed, after giving my dog Tzaddi her good-night biscuit, which she had great difficulty in chewing, and I saw the growth in her mouth. I proceeded to do my healing prayer work for various people I knew, which I always do before I sleep, when it suddenly occurred to me that I had been very foolish not to pray for Tzaddi, so I did some mental work for her, and then went to sleep.

"The alarm woke me at 7 A.M. and I quickly dressed, grabbed up Tzaddi, and drove to the veterinarian's, getting there a few minutes before 8 A.M. As I sat on the chair with Tzaddi, I suddenly remembered the treatment work of the night before, and looked into Tzaddi's mouth. *There was no tumor!* And yet I had seen it just six hours previously! I looked again, and examined her more carefully, but could not even see where the tumor had been! The area was smooth and clean, and looked exactly like the rest of her gum in the palate.

"The doctor arrived just then and verified my findings. I jubilantly took Tzaddi home, and have been most grateful to the Life Power for sparing my little pet the pain of an operation, or perhaps worse."

This is Ann Davies' story, and I have in my possession affidavits signed by the veterinarian, Dr. R. W. Short, confirming every statement Ann has made. I also have another affidavit, signed by five friends, witnesses to this amazing healing, two of whom I know personally, Felix V. Frazer and Dr. Paul Foster Case. The other three are Rosalie Gordon, Thelma Herkelrath and Bonnie Davies.

NEVER say that anything is impossible in the face of this and mounting evidence, from many sources, that the healing power of mind is *unlimited* in its functioning!

In some way that we still cannot comprehend, Ann Davies' picturization of her dog Tzaddi's mouth, as it had been before this growth appeared, reached the creative power within the consciousness of the dog and so activated it that an instantaneous healing took place!

This opens up a new field of speculation! Is it possible, because dogs have not been taught to speak, have not had their dog minds filled with words to which certain meanings have been given, that dogs or other animals, so treated, would respond more quickly and effectively than humans?

Remember, I have emphasized that we do not think in words. We think in pictures! The universal language is *feeling* because feeling can be communicated without words . . . it is extrasensory!

Certainly *something* happened, something definite, in answer to the *picture* Ann Davies held in her own mind. And what has happened once can happen again and again, when the same creative law is understood and applied to human beings as well as to animals.

Actually, I believe man is related to all forms of life, divided only by the body form he indwells. Some day man will develop the intelligence to communicate, understandably, with different forms of life, not through language, but through feeling!

Who knows? Perhaps the power of love united with the creative power and performed the healing. Intelligence operates in matter and upon matter but is *not* matter. This must really be the explanation. Mind is the basic ruler, and when mind takes charge, everything seemingly material must alter its form as mind directs! The magnet and the iron filings again!

There is a gold mine of health in this chapter. Get busy—and dig it out!

16

RIGHT MENTAL SUGGESTIONS CAN INFLUENCE PEOPLE

You've heard, all your life, about the power of suggestion: how easy it is to make a person ill by constantly suggesting to him that he doesn't look well. If enough people conspire to do this, the average individual can't take it. He actually gets sick.

The monotonous, persistent mental review of his crime often makes a lawbreaker confess. As a newspaperman, I have been in on many "third-degree sessions." I have seen detectives and prosecutors corner a single individual and shoot questions at him until his face was bathed in perspiration and he was nervous and jittery. It is the deadly repetition, the reiteration, the tap, tap, tap, through the power of suggestion which brings confessions.

A good salesman uses the power of suggestion all the time. A sale is effected by getting a prospect to think as you do; and unless you believe that the thing you are

selling is good, then obviously you can't make the other
fellow believe it.

That is just plain common sense. So for those of you
who may be selling, keep in mind what I have previously
said about knowing your article and selling yourself—that
is 99 per cent of the success of selling; the other 1 per cent
is leg work contacting the prospect.

You should realize that the bending of other people
to your will or getting them to do as you wish is simply
having them think as you think, and that is very easy. At
least, it always seems easy when you learn how it is done.

Elmer Gowing of Marion, Indiana, was the greatest
salesman of "anything" I have ever met in my life. It didn't
make any difference what the product or project or idea
was . . . Elmer could sell it. A civic club would put on a
drive of some kind which would be bogging down because its members couldn't sell it to the community. "Send
for Elmer!" someone would cry, and this long, lanky,
homely, good-natured middle-aged man would be sum-
moned. He would listen to the merits of the project and
would leave saying, "Is that all there is to it? Why don't
you give me something difficult?" Then Elmer would disappear, and in a few hours show up with enough backers
of the project to put it over. How he did it was Elmer's
secret.

One day the Junior Chamber of Commerce was putting on a home-talent show. Tickets had been printed up
late, and the local publicity on the event had not been
very good, with the consequence that by late afternoon of
the day before the performance very few tickets had been
bought.

"Where's Elmer?" demanded the J.C. President.

"Looks as if he's our only salvation—and I doubt if even Elmer can pull us out this time!"

The power of suggestion

Elmer was called in and given a packet of five hundred tickets, priced at a dollar apiece.

"Can you sell all these by tomorrow night?" he was asked.

Elmer looked at the bundle and then looked off into space. "I can," he said, "if you'll arrange with my boss for me to take off from work." The head of the insurance company who employed Elmer gave his consent. At four-thirty the next day, Elmer walked into the offices of the Junior Chamber of Commerce, his pockets bulging with bills and checks. "Looks as if you're going to have a full house tonight," he grinned. "They're all gone—and I could have sold more!"

This was too much for me. I had to get hold of Elmer's secret, so I went to see him. "How about having lunch with me tomorrow at the Spencer House?" said I. "I'll buy you the best meal in town, in return for the low-down on your selling power. Is it a deal?"

"It's so simple," said Elmer, "I'd be cheating you—but I like to eat."

The next day, as soon as we had finished lunch, I eyed Elmer, expectantly. "All right, Elmer," I appealed. "I've kept my end of the bargain. *Give!*"

In place of answering me, Elmer was playing with the table knife. He picked it up and examined it.

"I hadn't noticed before," he observed, "but this is uncommonly good silverware for a hotel to be using. I

190

could be wrong, but it looks like Gorham. Distinctive design. Wonder if the hotel bought it at an auction? I'll have to ask Manager Thornburg next time I see him." He handed the knife to me. "Notice how light it is ... real sterling, too ... this stuff is really high grade. ..."

I took the knife, a bit annoyed at this diversion because I was eager for Elmer to get on with his sales tip.

"You know, if I could buy a set of this silverware at a bargain price, I'd be tempted to do it," Elmer continued, as I held the knife and fixed my attention on it. "What do *you* think of it?"

"It *is* rather attractive," I conceded. "Light, as you say ... good design. ... I'm surprised myself at the hotel having silverware of this grade."

"Wouldn't you like to own a set like this?" Elmer asked. "That is, if the price were right ... ?"

"Well, I suppose I might," I agreed.

Elmer held out his hand. "I'll sell you that knife. Give me a quarter for it!"

Instinctively I caught myself reaching for my pocket to take out a quarter! Elmer had led up to this suggestion so cleverly, had intrigued my interest to the point where when he asked for the quarter, I felt almost impelled to buy a knife Elmer didn't own!

"That's all there is to it!" Elmer grinned. "Get your prospect to accept your product or proposition, whatever it is; place it in his hands, develop his appreciation of it, get him to agree with you, and remember the most important sales point of all—'possession is nine-tenths of the law.' Once an individual's mind *accepts* the product or the idea, and he has it in his possession, he doesn't want to give it up. It's harder for him to return it to you than it is to go down in his pocket and pay you for it!"

I can certainly testify to the truth of his statement about not wanting to give up a product. It seems silly, but I still felt impelled to hand Elmer a quarter and keep the knife! I was left with this urge, knowing the knife belonged to the hotel. This, to me, was selling, in the *nth* degree!

Those of you who are salesmen or who have your own businesses can increase business as a result of right thinking. When others tell you that business is bad, things are tough, going to the bow-wows, and hand you other negative thoughts of this nature—if you accept their thoughts and make them your own, your business *will* go to the bow-wows. Have no doubt about that. Then, as you talk to others, with your chin on your chest, your feet dragging and the front of a professional mourner, you tap them down, and the more you circulate and the more you talk (tap, tap, tapping with the same pessimistic story) and especially if you think and talk with an air of conviction, the more damage you do to yourself and those around you.

You are setting up thought, in reality fear thought, vibrations which are far-reaching. Fear thoughts are terrifically contagious and spread like wildfire. Conversely, as you direct your thoughts (visualizing) towards increasing your business, your sales, your profits, having no misgivings of your own (keeping your mind closed to the downward tapping thoughts of others) and putting enthusiasm, energy and action into your program—your business, your sales will automatically increase!

You must have the fire of enthusiasm!

You must keep in mind always that the intense fire of enthusiasm from within becomes a conflagration which affects all on your wave length as long as you radiate it. The vibrations you set up with your powerful rays of enthusiasm inspire others, raise them up, build and attract business . . . just as fear vibrations tap others down, repel and destroy.

It is an indisputable fact, irrespective of the times, that there is always business somewhere for the man who *believes* it exists and goes after it; but none for the person who is positive that none exists, and makes no endeavor to move.

Suggestion is one of the most powerful forces in the world. It has equal power in two directions—positive and negative—dependent on which direction you give it.

As a builder-upper, you can use suggestion upon yourself to excellent advantage. Now that you know the potency of thought, when you catch yourself taking on negative mental attitudes about anything you are doing or about the future, *stop everything!* Recognize at once the damage you are doing to yourself by permitting such thoughts to reside in your consciousness. Replace these wrong mental pictures with strong visual suggestions of the right kind. *See yourself* overcoming whatever difficulty you are facing, doing a better job, getting a better result tomorrow. Remember: the creative power within can only work on what you give it! A builder has to operate from a blueprint. If there are defects in the blueprint and he doesn't know about them, those defects will show up in the completed building. Unless you discover your wrong thinking, the wrong suggestions you are giving yourself each day, you'll attract what you are visualizing to you. Pass those suggestions on to your friends or associates and, if they accept them, they will help you produce the very conditions you have pictured!

What are we doing to the child mind?

Little children are more sinned against by parents and elders who are constantly giving them wrong suggestions than sinning:

"Don't go out dressed that way—you'll catch your death of cold!"

"Look out—you'll get run over!"

"Don't touch that—you'll break it!"

"I knew you'd do that! Can't you watch what you're doing?"

"Don't stay out late—something may happen to you!"

"Stay away from the water—you might get drowned!"

"You can't do that—better let me do it for you!"

"For heaven's sake, keep quiet! You don't know anything!"

"No, of course not—I don't trust you!"

"If you don't stop that, I'll call a policeman and have you locked up."

"You shouldn't ask questions like that—you're not old enough to know the answers!"

"So. you've done it again! Well, that's just what I expected!"

"Go away, you're a nuisance! I don't know why you were ever born!"

"Why, you little brat! I'm so mad I could kill you!"

You've heard these delightful suggestions and many, many more . . . and the only wonder is that children, subjected to this kind of highly emotionalized wrong thinking, turn out as well as they do!

The prize suggestion of all time, as reported by the Little Rock, Arkansas, *Gazette,* was made by an exasperated mother on a bus who was trying to feed her baby in the old-fashioned way. The baby, for some reason, was not interested in feeding, and finally the mother exclaimed: "If you don't take it, I'll give it to the bus driver!"

No doubt many parents are driven to distraction and beyond by the antics of their offspring, and feel called upon to use anything short of mayhem to get the children to mind them, but it is unwise to resort to fearsome and destructive suggestions as corrective measures. When a child is thus reprimanded, especially if he is in an emotionalized state, these wrong mental pictures of mishaps and misconduct and your own emphasizing of his defects take hold of his consciousness, causing him to develop a greater susceptibility toward the very things you want him to avoid or eliminate.

The homely or awkward or backward child starts out with natural handicaps, anyway, and if parents or elders constantly remind the child (repetition, reiteration!) how homely or awkward or backward he is, the child tends to become even more so. These are the very children who are in need of the finest kind of positive suggestions. Some teachers are now recognizing this need and are saying privately to unattractive or backward children, as they get the opportunity, "You're getting better looking every day! . . . You're doing much better!" Like little plants that have been lacking in nourishment, these children respond and unfold remarkably, in a short time. Try this method, reinforce it with the expression of *love* —and watch miracles happen!

Experiments in hypnotism have demonstrated, in many ways, the power of suggestion. Once the resistance of the conscious mind has been removed and the subconscious mind can be reached directly, it will respond instantly to whatever suggestions are given it, if what is suggested is within the moral standards of the individual. When suggestions repugnant to the basic character of the person are made, he either refuses to respond or comes out from under the hypnotic spell. It would require a series of suggestions designed to alter the present moral concepts before the individual would be willing to perform any act against his fixed standard of conduct. This clearly indicates that you do not change your acts until you change your mind, that what you have become through past experience and thought, you remain until something brings about a change in your own thinking.

You can be influenced while you sleep!

Psychologists are finding that many young and older people can be helped to overcome different faults and personal habits, inhibitions and inferiorities, if suggestions are made, at their bedsides, while they sleep. The subconscious mind never sleeps. It is always aware of what is going on, in and about you. Often, however, when you are mentally and emotionally disturbed and wish to control your mind and your feelings, you find it almost impossible to do so during your waking hours. If a loved one, with whom you have a sympathetic, understanding bond, could softly but positively suggest, after you have dropped off to sleep, that you *will* overcome your difficulties, these thoughts might find lodgment in your consciousness and aid you in developing a more positive attitude.

All life is really suggestion. You are constantly accepting or rejecting each experience that comes to you. If you accept it, your mind is acting upon it, for good or ill, dependent on the nature and character of the experience.

What you do and what you say, how you express your personality in the presence of others, is having a suggestive effect upon them, and they, in turn, are having a suggestive effect upon you. The more positive personality always dominates the less positive or emerges as the leader of a group. Negative people are attracted to positive people because they instinctively are seeking others stronger than themselves; they feel more secure in their presence; and if they are sincerely desirous of developing more positive qualities in themselves, they know this can best be done by emulating those who possess *positive* power.

Now, don't run out and accentuate the positive, just for the sake of being positive! I don't mean for you to start throwing your positive power around. But the well-balanced person, mentally and emotionally, has all the outward evidences of this balance in poise, self-assurance, charm and ease of expression and friendly interest in others. The manifestation of positive power is quiet. It is like the soft but powerful meshings of a hydromatic gear. You are scarcely aware it is operating, but the power is there ... and this power can be shifted from low to high, instantly, in an effortless manner. The man or woman who tries to dominate by force is misusing the power and revealing certain personality defects. Such people are really covering feelings of inadequacy and inferiority, and are trying by a surface show of power to compel attention. They may succeed for a time, but they can't hold success.

See yourself as you want to be!

Look in the mirror. Size yourself up. Are you the man or woman you want to be? If not, give yourself the suggestions that can help make you what you desire. See a mental picture of how you would like to appear to others, how you would like to express your personality *Superimpose* this mental picture upon the actual image of yourself, before you! See the changes you must bring about in yourself, as though they had already occurred! *Repeat* this visualization day after day, night after night. Work at it! Remember the power of repetition, reiteration ... tap, tap, tap!

If others criticize you or don't believe you are capable of doing what you want to do ... don't accept their suggestions! Analyze yourself to determine whether or not their criticisms are justified; and if they are, remove any resentment you may have had because of this criticism, give thanks that these defects were called to your attention, and get busy eliminating them so they will no longer hinder your upward progress. But maintain your belief in yourself! If you lose this, you lose everything. All success, big or small, starts with faith in self and faith in the creative power within. You must have it, and you must retain it—to go from where you are to where you want to be!

Say to yourself: "Each day I am going to improve and eventually I will remove the faults I discover in myself. Each day I am going to attain greater control of my mind and emotions. Each day I am going to overcome more of my fears and worries and other destructive thoughts. Each day I am developing greater health, happiness and prosperity. Each day I am going to find finer opportunities for serving others and the doing of worthwhile things. Each day. . . . !"

Take it up from here. Create your own tomorrows by your own *positive suggestions* as applied to yourself and your needs.

17

DANGER IN MISUSE OF TNT

High explosives must be handled, at all times, with caution. Your "detonating caps" are now set, you are getting ready to release this power within, so the time has now arrived to warn you what *not* to do, in connection with this mighty charge of T N T that you are carrying around with you, under your hat.

If you use this power wrongly, it will blow your hat skyhigh—and you, and all you hold dear, with it. Because you have been created a creature of free will and free choice, you can choose to use this power for evil . . . but you do so at your own great peril. Millions of human beings have destroyed themselves by so doing, and millions more will still do so before man thoroughly understands and gains control of this power in his life. This is the crime of the ages, that man has required so many untold centuries to even begin to gain an understanding of himself and this God-given power, which, rightly used, could long ago have brought man lasting peace and happiness; prosperity and health and everything good man could ever have desired!

Today, wrong thinking, the pent-up hates, resentments, greeds, fears, prejudices and other destructive feelings in all races of people are leading, inexorably, unless released by some miracle of new understanding of self and others, to the Cataclysm of the Ages!

You can only hold this power in leash for so long, and then it *must* manifest itself in some form, good or bad, in this outer world! Look about you. View the widespread unrest, the human suffering and privation in many countries, the economic pressures, the violent hatreds and prejudices, the mounting ill-will, the wars and rumors of wars—all man-made, through man's wrong thinking!

What can be done about it? How can this highly dangerous misuse of T N T be stopped, to avert unspeakable destruction of man and all he holds dear?

Something must be done! And you must be the one to do it! Action can no longer wait upon others. It must start with *you*. Every mind that is using this power as it should be used is adding something positive and constructive to universal thought. You can have great influence among your own friends, loved ones and community. Be realistic in your approach without being negative.

Whatever is to come, you can gain a great degree of guidance and protection for yourself by the right use of your own mind here and now. Actually, the power of mind to liberate or destroy man should be shouted to the housetops. The most tremendous educational program in all world history should be launched to reveal to man what he is doing . . . to himself!

History is replete with men who started out to use the power and were fast becoming headliners because of it. Then they succumbed to the temptation to use the power for selfish purposes, to take advantage of others, to gain domination over them. And while they succeeded for a time—some of them in a world-wide way—they all came to a tragic end. I have only to mention again such men as Nero, Julius Caesar, Mussolini, Hitler, Stalin, Lenin. . . . Think of all the misery they brought humanity, the power they once had, and how the evil they created through misuse of this power has lived after them, in some instances, even down through the ages!

Watch your own use of this power! Don't let your ego expand as you find that this power begins to elevate you!

Listen to the voice of your conscience! Ask yourself before each step you plan to take, "Am I making right use of this power? Am I employing it in a way that will bring harm to someone else, in time, or to me? Am I trying to advance too fast, before I am ready for the responsibilities and opportunities and experiences I am attracting?"

Make progress slowly but surely!

Yes, it is possible for you to gain success—temporary success—too quickly. This power within doesn't have the ability to analyze, or to determine your fitness to handle what you want, in the right way, when you get it. All it has the ability to do is to deliver to you what you instruct it to deliver, through the kind of mental pictures you give it. You must be the judge as to whether or not you are equal to the demands you make upon the power within, or it will produce results for you to which you cannot live up!

You know yourself better than any other person knows you. You know what you can and cannot do, within certain limitations. You know, for instance, if you are just out of college, that you still have to balance your education with experience, that you can't start out at the head of a business or industry. You know that you can't succeed on the strength of your diploma alone. I hope you know this much! But I have talked to hundreds of college men and women who have failed in business, who have not made a success of their lives, who have gone out into the world with the feeling that the world now owed them a living . . . that their education qualified them for anything they wanted. They operated this power, with the aid of a pleasing personality, to get into responsible positions; they went along swimmingly for a while, until their lack of experience began to catch up with them. Then they began to feel the pressure, they became less sure of themselves, they saw other men and women, with less education but more experience, climbing ahead of them. They couldn't take it, they grew jealous, resentful and finally apprehensive. What was wrong? They had everything—and yet it didn't seem to count for much in the world of reality—in the battle of life! Perhaps education itself must share part of the blame. . . . Perhaps youth has been taught to expect too much at the start.

Know yourself. Know what you want—be honest— what you feel you can handle. Picture yourself working to earn the right to possess what you are desirous of attaining. Don't wish upon yourself more than you are capable of doing at any time. You will grow naturally into finer and bigger opportunities, and the power within will supply you with everything you need, in addition to your own efforts, to get where you want to go, each step up the ladder of success and happiness.

Never use the power for selfish purposes!

It is a temptation to many people, coming into an awareness of this power for the first time, to attempt to use it for selfish purposes. The power will respond to your bidding, to whatever mental pictures you give it, whether your intentions are good or bad. You can picture taking advantage of some individual, and if you work toward that end, and if that person is too trusting and not alert to your designs, you may be able to put it over on him. But in the doing, you have created a *susceptibility*—a vibration—in your own consciousness which may attract to you that very same happening!

By such wrong manipulation of mind, you can, therefore, catch yourself in your own trap. What you plan to do to others you are really plotting to do to yourself, without realizing it, because "your own always comes back to you."

Are you willing to earn what you desire in life by your own efforts? What you gain, without effort, without deserving, you usually lose just as quickly. This is because the magnetic force which has attracted it is not sustained; little or no power has been built up around anything which has come to you in an unmerited manner (through wrong operation of mind), and consequently someone else, with wrong use of power, can take it away from you.

Like, remember, always attracts like. *If you don't want someone to do something to you, don't do it first to him!* This is a paraphrase of an old admonition but a word to the unwise should be the beginning of wisdom!

You can't get away with anything in mind, eventually. The law of compensation will see to that.

Up to now, only a small percentage of human beings, at any one time, have ever rightly used this T N T. But every time they have, it has brought them great personal happiness, achievement, health, prosperity—and even fame! The degree of happiness, achievement, health, prosperity and fame they have realized has been in proportion to the degree of use they have made of this power. This will always be so! Turn on a water faucet half-way, you will only get half the flow of water. Let only part of the power flow through you, and you diminish the returns it can bring to you.

Leaders who light the fuse of T N T by inflaming the hatreds and resentments and suspicions of great masses of people can wreak untold damage. Witness the Genghis Khans, Napoleons, Kaiser Wilhelms and Hitlers of history! There are always millions ready to be led for one who is willing and ready to lead . . . and to lead in the right direction! Mankind, as you know, has a tragic record of crucifying its Saviors.

The time for the right use of mind power is at hand

But the time is at hand for man to recognize and accept, irrespective of his religious or philosophic beliefs, his race or color, the spiritual power within him—"that something" which each man possesses and which, rightly directed, can bring to *all men* the peace and happiness and plenty and universal brotherhood man has so long been seeking.

It's *here*—right inside you—a part of you—in your

pocket; as it was in my pocket years ago, when I didn't realize, hadn't awakened to what I had; to what had always been mine . . . to what has always been in the world, available to all men in all ages; the treasure beyond all other treasures, the Holy Grail, the wisdom, the intelligence, the answer to all problems; but the curse of all curses, the most fiendish of all forces, if exploded in the wrong way by man's wrong thinking.

It's yours to use or to misuse. Now that you have it and know how to operate it—what are you going to do with it?

How you decide to use it, at any time, will change your world . . . and may change the whole world.

Danger: high explosive! Proceed with wisdom and with caution.

"If you believe it—it is so!" But *what* do you believe?

What you believe, and what the people of this world believe—will make the world of tomorrow! And the T N T of these beliefs will rock the earth!

18

QUESTIONS AND ANSWERS CONCERNING THE USE OF "THAT SOMETHING"

> *There are two things to aim at in life; first, to get what you want; and, after that, to enjoy it. Only the wisest of mankind achieve the second.*
>
> **LOGAN PEARSALL SMITH**

Through the years I have had many questions from men and women who have discovered "that something" within, the creative power of mind, and have been earnestly applying themselves to its study and use in their daily lives. Because some of these questions may be the very ones you would ask, I have selected the most representative ones to answer in this chapter with the hope that my answers will aid you in your further development and realization.

How can I keep my mind free from upsetting, weak, fear and worry thoughts, which come to me seemingly from outside?

Wrong emotional reactions to different experiences you have had have implanted in your mind fears that similar experiences may come to you. Subconsciously, because of these fears, anything that happens to you which is suggestive of former unhappy experiences produces these "upsetting, weak, fear and worry thoughts," as you describe them. The way to eliminate them is to release from your mind the emotional hold that past fears and worries have over you; and as you do this the power of these wrong thoughts to attract similar thoughts and reactions is proportionately reduced. In other words, the more you develop the *positive* attitude of mind, the less will you be influenced or disturbed by negative thoughts.

How can we have faith and ignore the fact that an enemy may be stalking us, ready to attack, or that the road we are following in the darkness may end in a precipice, or that water we are about to drink may contain pernicious germs? Few of us have developed the power of premonition so that it can be depended upon in emergencies or every-day life.

Blind faith is always dangerous and is often worse than no faith at all. Real faith possesses an "inner *knowing* quality" about it. Such faith is based upon an intelligent awareness of the factors upon which you are basing your faith. You are not using your intelligence when you proceed, without caution, in an area where you may encounter an enemy, or come upon a precipice or possibly infested water. Faith was never intended as a substitute for intelligent action. It was and is designed to augment your own intelligence—to activate the creative powers within to attract what you want and need to you, in association with your own efforts in that direction.

If you picture in mind, with faith, that you can safely avoid or meet an encounter with the enemy, or be guided without mishap along a road in the darkness, or be forewarned when you are about to do anything harmful, such as the drinking of contaminated water—the creative power within follows your orders and gives you the "hunches," the impulses, urges and "premonitions" which serve to protect you.

You say that, in case of great danger, the subconscious makes us choose the right move. Yet, everybody, including myself, knows cases of people who, caught in a fire, have abandoned their most precious belongings,. while dragging out worthless pieces of furniture—or they have run the wrong way when the right one was open. How do you account for this?

Your subconscious will *not* "choose the right move" for you in an emergency, unless prepared by *right thinking* to do so! If you have always been afraid of fire and have not pictured what you would do in case of fire, you will be paralyzed by that fear when you find yourself caught in a fire, unable to receive any right direction from your subconscious. Remember: what comes out of your mind is only that which has gone into it at some previous time . . . because you have created your world by your own past reaction to it. In your desire to save something from the fire, because you have never pictured the things worth saving in event of fire, you hysterically grab up anything. Because you have never pictured what exits you would take in case of fire, you have only one frenzied thought—to get out—not the *way* to get out! Start now in preparing your mind to meet *any* emergency. I do a great amount of traveling, stopping in all types of motels and hotels. I have no fear of fire, but as an intelligent precaution the first thing I do, upon arriving at my destination, is to locate the exits nearest my room, the position of the fire escapes and stairways. I even test the fire-escape doors to see if they happen to be locked, or windows leading out onto fire escapes, to determine if they may be jammed. (In many instances I have found conditions that would not have permitted escape, through locked doors and windows that would not open.) I picture in my mind the layout of the room and whether a right or left turn, on leaving it, takes me to the nearest exit, so I could find it in the dark, if necessary. This check-up and observation takes me five to ten minutes, and then I dismiss it from my conscious mind, knowing that if a fire should break out, I will instantly be made aware of the right moves to make. In addition, I decide just what articles I will take with me so that I won't be confused in trying to determine this at a time of fire when my mind needs to be free to meet the existing situation. Your subconscious, "that something" within, will never fail you if you properly instruct it and liberate your consciousness from fear.

You say the subconscious is all-intelligent and practically infallible, if I understand you correctly. Then "how come" that the subconscious can be influenced by wrong, unwarranted or pernicious thoughts or happenings from outside?

Suggestion! Your subconscious is instantly reactive to everything that happens to you in your outer world, if you accept it with your conscious mind. Never forget: whatever you take in, your mental pictures of experiences, is stored in your subconscious. That's why I have warned you, again and again, to beware of using your T N T the wrong way. Learn to control your wrong reaction to the things that happen to you. Don't keep on passing in to your subconscious mind fear and worry thoughts about conditions and circumstances around you. If you do, you are simply ordering that power within to keep on attracting this kind of things to you, because that is all you are picturing for it. You are creating the pattern, over and over, of what has already happened, by so doing. Your subconscious is infallible in its following of whatever instructions you give it with your conscious mind. It possesses an intelligent awareness, but it has no reasoning power. This is possessed alone by your conscious mind. So don't depend on your subconscious to do your thinking for you. It can *perceive* for you, if you direct it so to do, and bring you knowledge of things you need to know about, or put you in touch with sources for such knowledge . . . but it is subservient, at all times, to your desires, your decisions, your free-will choices.

You say, "think the other fellow is a nice, decent man and he will become friendly." But suppose you know definitely he is a scoundrel and a blackguard. Do you recommend one should still deceive himself in such a case?

I certainly do not recommend self-deception. If you know a certain person is "no good," as you imply, and not worthy of trust, you should, of course, be on your guard in any relations or contacts with him. Too often, however, individuals have made mistakes of a social or personal or criminal nature and have been so condemned by a self-righteous society that they are not permitted to make atonement for these mistakes. We expect ill from them and we get what we expect. Defensively and defiantly, these people show us their worst sides because we bring this worst side out by our own attitudes. It never hurts to give any individual the "benefit of the doubt," to appeal to his or her "best side," to give him credit for the good you see in him. Since like always attracts like, if a person feels that you are sincere, if you demonstrate your faith in him—it is more than likely he will attempt to justify this faith by returning good to you. Picture yourself being protected from the wrong thinking or wrong doings of others. Don't let yourself fear that others will take advantage of you, because this very fear will make you susceptible. Many times people have said to me, "I can't understand what you see in So-and-So" or "How can you get along with So-and-So?" It's simply because I look for the good, while these other people put up barriers which are resented. Consequently, they awaken wrong reactions in individuals who would treat them differently if they, themselves, were treated differently. Even a dog can instinctively tell how you really feel about him, however much you pretend otherwise. Wouldn't you treat human beings better than dogs? If we deny others a chance to make a come-back, what hope is there for us?

I believe you said, somewhere, that a person with a workable idea, and thoroughly convinced of its soundness, seldom has any difficulty in getting money to finance it. And yet, how many inventors, deeply convinced of the value of their inventions, have died in the poorhouse?

I have decried and denounced the unwillingness of many scientists and other intelligent people to accept or even consider new ideas. With regard to telepathy, I have stated that practically all the great electrical scientists—including Edison, Steinmetz, Tesla and Marconi—were greatly interested in telepathy. So was Dr. Alexis Carrel, who believed in it and declared that a study should be made of it by scientific men, just as physiological phenomena are studied. But despite this interest and the investigations of scientists like Dr. J. B. Rhine at Duke University, the London Society for Psychical Research, the American Society and others, which have produced a mountain of evidence, there are still scientists who belittle this work. They do not wish to consider any idea which might upset their already established theories. It is this "closed mind" attitude which the average inventor encounters. An inventor is often a quiet, introspective individual who has had not too much experience in facing the world. He can *visualize* what he desires to invent with faith and confidence that the creative power within will help produce it for him, but he cannot visualize, with equal faith and confidence, gaining recognition and resources for his invention. This, to him, is a different world. He submits his invention to a few prospects, and if he is rebuffed he often becomes discouraged, even despondent, and pictures failure.

Under these conditions, the inventor is working the creative power against himself. Because you are a "successful visualizer" in one phase of your life activity is no indication that you can be or are equally successful in other phases. The same right thinking must apply to all and any of your desires or needs. Some men and women naturally possess what is called a "money consciousness" —they *see* themselves making money, everything they touch turning to money—and the power within helps them make and attract money. But many of these same people are just as unsuccessful in other departments of their lives, as is evidenced by ill health, inability to get along with others, lack of personal happiness and contentment, and all manner of other deficiencies. Each inventor should face his problem of selling and marketing his invention, of getting financing for it, with the same enthusiasm, the same persistence, the same energetic application of his visualizing powers that he has given to the development and creation of the invention itself. If he does, he will certainly succeed in his enterprise, as any and all succeed who make proper use of "that something" within.

How can we distinguish real hunches as opposed to merely our wishful thinking, the expression of desires and passions of our conscious mind, at a given moment?
This ability to discriminate between a real hunch and an intuitive flash or premonition comes with prac-

tice. True hunches enter the conscious field of your mind without any reflection or premeditation. You just suddenly "know" or "feel" something, you get a strong urge to do or not to do something, to be on your guard, to check or investigate. Self-analysis will help you determine whether or not an impulse which you receive has been created by you through wishful thinking, an excessive desire or passion, as you characterize it. You should know yourself well enough to assume an impersonal attitude and say: "I'm just kidding myself. I wanted to get that kind of an impression and I've stimulated my imagination to give it to me. I don't recognize this as a true hunch. My fears have dramatized themselves and given me the false feeling that something is going to happen." You will soon detect a difference in *feeling*, when a real hunch hits you.

Your remembrance of how you felt when you got this real hunch will enable you to recognize other genuine intuitive flashes and to disregard such other feelings as come to mind which originate as a result of your own fears or pampered desires. You must *believe* that your inner mind can and will serve you by giving you intuitive flashes, as needed, or else the power within cannot function in this manner for you. Some people say, "I don't believe in hunches—and I've never had any, that I recall." This mental attitude has blocked off such intuitive impulses as might have been received. Learn to control your own excessive desires, things you know are not good for you, eliminate your fears—and you will then put up less and less resistance to the reception and recognition by you of guidance and protection from your faculty of intuition.

My problem is not in the form of money, business or gaining fame. I have the problem of stuttering and stammering which is foremost in my mind. Since studying your philosophy, I have noticed some improvement in my speech. I realize that results in conditions like this do not come overnight—although I would like to have rather fast results. Could you give me any hints as to how to hasten the subconscious in its wonderful work on my problem?

Go back in your life to the time, if you can recall it, when you started stuttering. What emotional experience brought on this condition? Were you criticized at a particularly sensitized moment by your parents or by someone? Was there a dominant member of your family who repressed you, in whose presence you were afraid to express yourself? Did you feel overshadowed by someone— or did you suffer such a fright that you temporarily found it impossible to speak? Somewhere in your past is the original cause of your present difficulty. Find it and you can then release yourself from the hold this emotional reaction has had upon you. As a further aid, since stuttering and stammering are usually associated with a degree of self-consciousness and overanxiety . . . wait a few seconds before speaking. Take a breath, and *picture* in your mind what you are going to say before putting it into words. If you are groping in mind for words, your full attention is distracted from your speech centers and, as a result, your speech is halting and sometimes broken. Recovering your ability to articulate each word correctly is largely a matter of proper "timing" and visualization. Co-ordinate the two, and you will soon overcome this condition.

I firmly believe in your teachings. You state that one should use this power for good and not evil. This I believe 100 per cent—so that is why I am asking, would it be evil to use this power for gambling? I'm not a professional gambler but like many people, I do it to some extent. Would it be harmful to use this power for gambling on either a large or small scale?

Frederick Marion, noted seer, author of the book, *In My Mind's Eye,* in which he tells of many of his experiences with extrasensory perception, his developed ability to sense the thoughts of others, to foresee the future, also tells of his attempts to use his powers for determining when to buy and sell stocks. For a time he was successful; then his powers commenced to fail him. He could not control his human desire to try to force an answer when so much money was riding on every hunch that he needed, to "guess right." Every gambler who has used his intuition, has had it fail him under pressure. Most gamblers I have known have died broke or have had many more downs than ups. They never know when to stop—a success eggs them on to new losses. If they played the "game of life" straight, without tension and strain, their intuitive faculties would serve them more regularly and dependably. Life, in a sense, is a gamble . . . you are betting on yourself to win . . . and I would rather bet on myself than on a wheel of chance any day. Gambling is evil when you hurt yourself and others by doing it. Only those should gamble who can afford to lose. Unhappily, few of this type ever gamble. What is your classification? Why not bet on yourself instead? The risks are less and the gains, over a lifetime, are much greater—and more satisfying.

Can you suggest a formula or plan to aid me in sorting out the best for me of several things I could do and want to do—commercially?

No one can really do this for you but yourself. In your periods of meditation, say to your inner mind, the creative power within: "Determine for me wherein my best business opportunities lie—what abilities and past experiences I can crystallize and capitalize upon in my future." Give this picture to your subconscious, and then go about your business, in the faith and confidence that at the right time, through an intuitive flash or a sudden awareness, you will *know* the direction in which to go and how to go about it. You can depend upon it. The answer will be forthcoming.

Some writers claim that you do not learn by experience. Please explain what you mean by "learning by experience."

Learning by experience how *not* to do things as well as how to do them. Learning to profit by the experiences of others. Why should you make the same mistakes others have made if you observe in advance that a path they have taken has led them up a "dead-end street?" Use your intelligence as well as your faith in facing life and its problems.

I am stymied or bogged down with "clutter-clutter." How can I get out from under the feeling of chaos?

By eliminating your confused and disturbed thinking. You have formed the bad habit of paying too much attention to little, unimportant, insignificant details and happenings, building them up into mountains and obstacles in your mind. They thus have become, as you have described, a lot of "clutter-clutter," milling around in your conscious mind, obstructing real thoughts and ideas that are trying to get through to you. You have a constant feeling of impending chaos only because these disturbed thoughts give you the sensation of being "overwhelmed or engulfed" by them. Throw them out, through an act of will and it will be "goodbye, chaos—welcome, law and order" in your mind.

What place does imagination have in the scheme of things if it is liable to mislead one's thinking?

Right direction of imagination, like anything else, makes it a tremendous power for good, instead of harm. Imagine good things coming to you—and good eventually comes as you have pictured it, through imagination; imagine ill, and you will get bad results in due time.

What is imagination?

Imagination is that faculty of mind which enables you to form in your inner consciousness a mental image or picture of what you want. It is the stimulator of thought, the activator of the creative power within, the means of making your desires specific.

How do you picture or think of the God Power or Presence within—when you pray? Can you just pray to a feeling of inner power?

Each person has his own concept of God, and what ever concept that is most satisfying, meaningful and help ful to you is the one you should use in your meditations and prayers. I certainly do not picture God, when I pray, as anthropomorphic in nature, seated on some vast throne somewhere in heavenly space. I have long since outgrown this childhood concept. Today, I have the conviction that a part of God, the Great Intelligence, indwells each human soul—you and me. You can recall how close you have felt and still feel toward a loved one. As you think of that loved one *now*, you bring him or her instantly to mind and you feel the bond of closeness which exists. In much the same way, let these feelings of closeness and intimacy come to you from God. You know your loved one exists as you think of him or her; you haven't the slightest doubt about it. Then, let yourself feel and know that God exists, and you will sense the God Presence within—the power that will never let you down, to whom you can go in meditation and prayer, and from whom you may expect right answers.

Would you kindly tell me what techniques one may use to blot out unhappy experiences of the past and how to forgive one's loved ones?

By realizing that you are doing yourself great harm by retaining the bitter memory of these experiences— that you are not hurting those who have hurt you nearly so much as you are hurting yourself. Review what has happened in your mind, then *picture* in your mind's eye what you now realize you should have said and done. Assume your share of the blame and responsibility . . .

and, however justified you may feel for holding malice against your loved ones, *let go* now of all your hate and resentment. Know and believe that the law of compensation will take care of them, eventually, for their misdeeds and wrong thinking. Realize that as long as your attention is fixed on the past and its unhappiness and on losses you can never recover, you are holding yourself back from receiving new resources, new opportunities and new experiences of a happy nature. Remember: like attracts like: and you have been attracting a repetition of miserable feelings, as you have lived these experiences over and over. It isn't worth it. It will destroy all health and happiness in time, unless abandoned—and a new, positive attitude assumed.

Is there a difference between prayer and meditation?
Yes. Meditation is preparation for prayer, through relaxing the physical body of all tension, making the conscious mind passive and then, with your attention turned inward, entering upon prayerful visualization of those things you need and desire.

If your parents keep reminding you from childhood to the present day that you cannot succeed—how can you remove this block successfully?
This is a fine heritage for parents to pass on to a child into adulthood—a series of "you can't succeed" pictures! Your first step toward the liberation of your consciousness from this parental bondage is the realization that the moment you reject their negative concepts of you, these wrong pictures can no longer retain their hold

over your mind. You have to *believe* that you can't succeed before you will fail. Put out of your mind all resentment of what your father and mother have done to you. As long as you remain bitter you will keep these unhappy pictures and their influence alive in your consciousness. Let go of this bitterness, and these pictures will be deprived of all nourishment in mind and die of starvation. There is much remaining in life for you that is good and worthwhile. Claim it—through right visualization and the exercise of faith in yourself and in the unfailing power of "that something" to bring you what you have long desired and deserved!

Let me determine if I understand you: you form the picture of your desire, consciously, and then, while being very quiet, it is reflected back to you, probably only for the fraction of a second! Is this reflection—seeing it—in your mind's eye? And is this what must *happen, before the creative power within can be impelled to bring you effective results?*

Yes, you have described the process very well. You first create the mental image of what you desire, and then project it upon the inner mental screen through an act of will, letting yourself feel a strong desire for the materialization of this picture in real life, having faith, at the same time, that what you have visualized has already been achieved in mind and is even now on the way to you!

With the world in such a turmoil, how can a person keep from worry and fear? How can the unpleasant happenings be kept out of mind?

By refusing to personalize those happenings which have no direct relation to you. Recognize that fear and worry will not correct the world situation, nor even help you solve any of your own problems. In fact, fear and worry are demoralizing and devitalizing. In time, they can destroy self-confidence, health and happiness. Realize that you, yourself, are reasonably well and happy *now*— and that your greatest contribution to yourself and others will always be the maintenance of a positive, cheerful, optimistic attitude. Stop living in a "hope for the best and fear the worst" state of mind. The worst hardly ever happens, and when you aim at the best, things always turn out better than you have thought possible.

What is the quickest way to relax?

I presume the quickest way would be to hit yourself on the head with a hammer—but the after-effects wouldn't be too desirable. The next quickest and the safest and sane way is to get off by yourself, if possible, sit down in an easy chair or stretch out on a cot, and *let go* of your physical body with your conscious mind . . . lift arms and legs and drop them . . . let the chair or bed support your entire body. You will feel a lightness and sense of buoyancy come over you. Then, with your body relaxed, let go of all feelings of tenseness in mind, brought about by high pressure, fear, worry or other emotional disturbances. Visualize a blank mental screen . . . a quiet pool of water . . . a calm, restful landscape . . . anything which suggests a peaceful, motionless area. The instant you have done this, you are relaxed; and it should take you less than two minutes—with practice—to let go in this manner.

Can you induce dreams, by suggestion, and cause your intuition to make known certain information to you in this way?

Yes, much knowledge can be revealed to you through dreams, and the creative power within often uses a dream as a medium through which to present information you need to have of past, present or future events. Of course, the difficulty of correct interpretation often enters in because many dreams are caused by disturbed physical and mental states (such as indigestion, fear, worry, suspicion, resentment, etc.). There is a tendency, when the conscious mind is made passive, through sleep, for the troubles of the day to dramatize themselves in distorted dream form—and this type of dream is seldom significant. It may reveal, to the psychiatrist, the causes of your fears and apprehensions and other emotional instabilities, but little or nothing to you. However, there are other times when you are projected ahead into the future, and your intuitive faculties bring you vivid dreams, in whole or in part, of events coming toward you in time . . . events for which the causes already exist . . . causes you may have set up in yourself through your reaction to past experiences. These dreams deserve your most careful analysis, for they may give you a clue as to how you should prepare to meet or to avoid a developing situation. These dream warnings, properly evaluated, can enable you to change your thinking and thus change the possible happenings themselves.

Upon retiring, if you desire an answer, during sleep, to a pressing problem—suggest to "that something" within that it bring you the answer in this manner. With practice, you can often induce the reception of information you need, in dreams. Many people say, "I decided to sleep on it—and I woke up with the answer!"

If man is master of his fate, responsible to no one but himself, how can you resolve this and the fact that life has been at work in a thousand ways, functioning as a "going concern" before he was born? It certainly appears at every point we are involved in processes, functions and activities over which we are unable to exercise any significant control. How do we answer this?

Man *should* be master of his fate. He was so designed and given the potentiality through a creative power within, capable of carrying him to inconceivable heights. But man, thus far, has not made too intelligent use of this power, en masse. Individually, however, man's achievements have approached the sublime. Consider Helen Keller, who rose above seemingly hopeless handicaps of deafness, dumbness and blindness—expressing her personality and her great soul through her impaired physical instrument as an inspiration to all mankind. Surely she is a "master of her fate." Give a thought to Steinmetz, the electrical wizard, who was born with a misshapen head, a hunchback, spindly legs, an over-all frail body. But the oddly formed head housed a great brain. Those who knew Steinmetz say that they lost all consciousness of his body, the brilliance of the man caused it to fade from sight. Another "master of his fate."

Think, too, of Beethoven, whom nature endowed with an ugly face and a defect which should have been fatal to anyone who aspired to write music—he became deaf! And yet the mind of Beethoven brought forth some of the noblest music ever written, music that will live forever and bring joy to millions still unborn. Few human beings realize, when they thrill to Beethoven's greatest work, his *Ninth Symphony*, that this great composer never heard a single note of it! Surely, this giant of music was "master of his fate." And hundreds and thousands of other men and women, calling upon "that something"—the creative power within—have surmounted all the "processes, functions and activities" which they found in existence when they arrived here, and which ordinarily might have been thought to be against them; obstacles to their attainment of any success.

No. Man has not been cast adrift in this world, a victim of circumstances and forces beyond his control. He possesses, in his inner consciousness, all the power he needs for *self-mastery*. Man has but to discover it and learn to use it. That is all.

19

SHARE YOUR GOOD
FORTUNE WITH OTHERS

When you get hold of a good thing, pass it on. That's the way to win friends and attract more people to you. Don't be selfish. When you get the opportunity, help others to understand TNT and to make it do the same for them that it has done for you. Every time you give others a lift, you give yourself a bigger one.

Some people, who don't understand and don't want to understand, may say you are conceited, self-centered, or selfish; but don't let this disturb you. Those are the scoffers . . . those who would put rocks in your road and otherwise impede your progress. You'll always encounter this type on the highways and byways of life. They are not going anywhere, and want to take you along v th them. Those who understand will want what you ha ₊ to give them and will be helpful, eager to serve you .. to work with you. The intelligent ones, as they observe the headway you are making will begin to study you ᵗo determine what you have that they haven't—and try to discover your secret.

I have given you a grip on it; hold it to you tightly and start moving forward.

George Jean Nathan, one of America's foremost dramatic critics, in a compilation of *Living Philosophies*, declares he has never known a man who succeeded in life, in a material way, who did not think of himself first, last and all the time. Naturally, I don't know just how Nathan meant that, but I am sure he did not mean that a successful man is selfish to the point where he isn't helpful to others; because if you follow the theme as I have outlined it, and get on the road to success, you will not be led to act ruthlessly.

You won't have to batter others down to get where you want to go; you won't have to climb over their dead bodies; you won't have to doublecross your friends and business associates; you won't have to reach your goal through connivance and pretense and deceit You'll get there with your head up and your feet firmly on the ground. And what you have been able to do once, you'll know how to do again and again—and do better each time.

This is what the creative power of mind, working in and through you, can and will do for you. As you progress, you will find that you'll wish to do charitable things, good things, for other people; performing services, little acts of kindness and thoughtfulness, going an extra mile or two to help the other fellow when you can, in appreciation of what has been done for you. As and when you do this, you'll observe that your friendly acts will bring about a willingness in the other fellow to do something for you. There is nothing selfish about this—it's just a matter of cause and effect.

André Ampère knew the law. He called it the law of attraction as applied to electrical magnetism: *"Parallel currents in the same direction attract one another."* Simple, isn't it? And when you are out of tune and antagonistic, you put others out of tune and make them antagonistic because: *"Parallel currents in opposite directions repel one another."* It's the old, old, true story, boiled down to three big little words: *"Like begets like!"*

When you perform a service you will be paid huge dividends. There is no mystery about it, it's just so!

Tap—tap—tap! Start doing what you've been told to do, over and over again, until your technique of right thinking is perfected.

There is strength in teamwork. Get others in on this kind of thinking with you! The *esprit de corps* pounded into those of us who were in the Army in the First World War made the American forces what they were. This same spirit is responsible for the terrific job our boys did in the Second World War; and inspired teamwork in any battle will provide the enthusiasm, the confidence and the determination to move always forward.

If you accept what I am telling you in the spirit in which it is given, and put it into execution, you will be unbeatable. And by getting in tune and getting others on the track, the world is yours!

"When Fear rules the will, nothing can be done, but when a man casts Fear out of his mind, the world becomes his oyster.

"To lose a bit of money is nothing, but to lose hope—

*to lose nerve and ambition—that is what makes men crip-
ples."*
Herbert N. Casson

Charles M. Schwab once said: "Many of us think of
salesmen as people traveling around with sample kits
Instead, we are all salesmen, every day of our lives We
are selling our ideas, our plans, our energies, our en
thusiasm to those with whom we come in contact."

So it is with every endeavor, and especially is this
true of selling commodities, because there you *must* con
tact people

And when I say "contact," I mean contacting them
face-to-face. The day of order-taking is once more disap-
pearing. It never really was here . . . because there is no
substitute for seeing prospects face-to-face. But even more
so in the days to come, the only persons who will achieve
outstanding success will be those who get out and "beat
the bushes" and meet the people. The others will sink.

You cannot get around this fundamental law, "the
survival of the fittest." Therefore forget about order-taking, and keep in mind that the only way you can close a
sale is to make the prospect think as you think! The best
way will always be face-to-face contact. You have got to be
in his presence, you have got to see his reactions—"the old
law of cause and effect"—and you have got to adapt yourself to the conditions as they confront you with the individual prospect.

If you are intent on making a sale (and you must be
if you are going to succeed) keep in mind my theme. The
subconscious mind will be giving you ideas, hunches,
inspirations, a perfect flood of them, which will guide you
correctly. They will point out the way to get into a busy

man's presence—into the privacy of his very self; and, when you get there, to stand on both feet.

Be alert. Make your prospect feel your personality. Know what you are talking about. Be enthusiastic. Don't quail!

You are just as good as he is, and besides you may have something which he hasn't, and that is utmost confidence, utmost faith in the article you are selling. On the other hand, if he is a success, he also has personality. Therefore, be sure to put the contact on a fifty-fifty basis. Do not belittle him: do not let him belittle you. Meet on common ground. Make him like you, and when he likes you and you him, success is on its way. Hold in mind from the start that you are going to sell him. . . . You are going to sell him!

Your main, over-all theme in life, of course, is: "I am going to succeed in everything I undertake! . . . I am going to succeed in everything I undertake!" (Repetition, reiteration. Tap–tap–tap! Always tapping, pushing forward. Repeating, repeating—seeing yourself doing it, over and over—visualizing, "I can! . . ." "I will! . . ." "I believe it—and it is so!")

Get your friends interested. Form study groups. Exchange experiences. Discuss your failures. Find out what mistakes you made. Pick up the pieces and try again. Criticize each other. Determine why certain plans didn't work out. Share the news and the joy of your successes! Conduct experiments in telepathy, in developing your powers of visualization, concentration, intuition. Demonstrate the value of T N T to your friends, family and business associates as their interest in this power develops.

With a nucleus of interest in T N T eventually established in each community, with large numbers of men and women studying and applying the power of right thinking . . . great changes will begin to take place in the minds and hearts of people and the world!

Each owner of this book can set up his own nucleus and start to work with his own interested friends and associates. The secret is all here . . . ready to be unfolded to each reader, each student.

It helps your development to work with an understanding friend or loved one, it gives you added impetus. You can each check, assist, and encourage the other. The more you talk about inner power of mind, the more thought and study you give to it, the more it becomes manifest in your life.

Keep tapping . . . never let up . . . never give up . . . because the answer exists for the solution of every problem you have had or could have—in your own mind!

And remember, always, to share your good fortune with others. You will be rewarded a hundredfold . . . a thousand . . . as your sharing continues, because good compounds itself—multiplies, keeps on multiplying . . . expanding . . . returning more and more good to the original giver.

Persevere, have faith, visualize, *you can't miss!*

20

NOW YOU HAVE THE POWER—
USE IT!

> *I am the master of my fate:*
> *I am the captain of my soul.*
>
> WILLIAM ERNEST HENLEY

Tap–Tap–Tap–Tap
As a man thinketh in his heart—so is he.
Tap–Tap–Tap–Tap
I know it, I believe it and it's so.
Tap–Tap–Tap–Tap
T N T—IT ROCKS THE EARTH!

This book will do everything for you that is claimed, but you must reread it and reread it until every sentence, every word is thoroughly understood; and then you must apply the principles and mechanics with your whole heart and soul. Make them a part of your daily life and when you put into practice the ideas offered, you will find that they will work just as they've always worked and always will. If you are in deadly earnest with yourself, you will find the entire scheme very simple.

After you have studied the book and have reflected upon the ideas set forth, you will appreciate the tremendous force which lies in the science of *thought repetition* and *positive action.*

You can, by repetition of the same thought "tap" yourself upward or downward—depending on whether you have depressed or constructive thoughts. And as you build yourself powerfully, you will find that you can influence others by your thoughts.

Therefore, let me again admonish you to exercise great care that you do not misuse your power. Keep your mind filled with good, constructive thoughts, and then act with all the energy you possess as the ideas come to you.

Stop looking backward. You know where you've been: you want to know where you are *going!* Train your mind's eye on the future. This is the glorious land in which your opportunities lie. Gradually, as you become more and more adept in the control and direction of "that something," the creative power within, your intuition will bring you glimpses of your future.

The future is an extension of time and causation beyond the reach of the five physical senses

Study this statement; read and reread it, and the realization will come that the causative forces you set in motion by your thinking today are producing their effects for you in the world of tomorrow. Nature abhors a vacuum. Something is happening everywhere at all times . . . and everything that is happening is repercussing on everything around it. A great scientist said it all in one sentence when he declared: "The only thing permanent in the universe is change." Millions of cells in your body are dying and millions of new cells are being born every day. Old ideas are dying and fading away as new ideas originate in mind. You are not the same today as you were yesterday—in body or thought!

Many great seers, throughout the ages, have been able to look into the future and intuitively sense what was coming toward the peoples of the world—in time— as a result of their own thinking.

Alfred, Lord Tennyson left this earth in 1892, but listen to his prophetic voice as he says:

> For I dipt into the future, far as human eye could see,
> Saw the Vision of the world, and all the wonder that
>   would be;
> Saw the heavens fill with commerce, argosies of magic
>   sails,
> Pilots of the purple twilight, dropping down with
>   costly bales;
> Heard the heavens fill with shouting, and there rain'd
>   a ghastly dew
> From the nations' airy navies grappling in the central
>   blue. . . .
> Till the war drum throbbed no longer and the battle
>   flags were furled
> In the Parliament of Man, the Federation of the
>   world.

Can you read this and any longer doubt that Man can develop the power to "see" the future? There is unimagined power in T N T as it applies to the present and the future! What you create in mind, at any moment, becomes a reality from that instant on, unless you countermand it by a change in thought. Even then, the harm of wrong thinking goes out from you and joins with similar thoughts of others, existing in the "mental ether." Universal consciousness teems with the thoughts, good and bad, of the billions of human beings on this planet. The stupendous vibrations from these thoughts are having their effect on individual consciousness, as individuals tune in and out of different levels of this mass thinking.

Can we gain an understanding of each other's minds and emotions in time to build a better world? Can we adjust our grievances and our differences between friends and relatives and fellow men at home and abroad? Or will, as Tennyson suggests: ". . . the nations' airy navies" have to "grapple in the central blue," sending down their rain of "ghastly dew"?

How long must man continue his wrong thinking which leads only to the eventual destruction of all he holds dear, before the war drum throbs no longer and the battle flags are furled and there is established "the Parliament of Man, the Federation of the world"?

This question will be answered in a positive manner when enough individuals come to realize that T N T rocks the earth, either for man's good or ill, depending on how it is used!

Strength of mind must, one day, equal and surpass strength of arms!

Think what the direction of this T N T power in constructive channels by all human beings could mean to mankind—overnight! All problems would instantly be solved, inventions of benefit to humanity would liberate the entire human race from bondage of every kind, and true understanding and tolerance of others would come into existence! Then each would bend to his particular task in service to himself and others, for, as James Russell Lowell says:

> *No man is born into the world whose work*
> *Is not born with him; there is always work*
> *And tools to work withal, for those who will,*
> *And blessed are the horny hands of toil...*

Idle hands always finds trouble: no one is truly happy who has not worthwhile work to do. You must come to know what you want and how to get what you want to find contentment and success in life! But you must also give thought to the other man's right to free expression and attainment of his rightful desires.

You are not in this world alone; you are here to help others even as you will be helped. You are important to yourself, to your friends and loved ones, to your community, your nation. What you are doing in life is important. The work of every individual counts in the great scheme of things. No good effort is ever lost.

When you do the best you can each day, whatever your job or responsibility may be, you are improving yourself and the conditions around you.

Knowing that you possess this power within, and knowing how to draw upon it, you need not waste your time and energy worrying about national and international conditions that are beyond your influence.

Make your influence felt where you live ... and you will be doing your part and inspiring others to do theirs.

Remember: *every thought, kept ever constant, leads to action, and results follow.*

So keep this book always close at hand. Reread it, study it, and reread and study it as frequently as possible.

Practice, practice, practice—tap, tap, tap! Inspire others by your daily demonstration of right thinking! By so doing, you will be contributing your share towards making the world in which you live a better, safer, happier place. And what goes out from you that is good, goes out to the world at large, as well—and finds its affinity with right thinking people everywhere.

In the beginning, all things were good. Man, himself, made them bad. You do evil and evil will be done you. You do good and you will receive good in return. You can be what you wish and have everything you want, provided you are willing to pay the price in time, thought, effort and energy. You now have the key—may you make it work!

"That something," rightly used, is:

TNT—IT ROCKS THE EARTH

It is the POWER WITHIN—YOU!